Obsessive Compulsive Anonymous
Recovering From Obsessive Compulsive Disorder

Second Edition

Obsessive Compulsive Anonymous World Services, Inc.

New Hyde Park, New York

ISBN 0-9628066-2-5

Library of Congress Catalog Card No.: 99-93043

03 02 01 00 99

5 4 3 2 1

Manufactured in the United States of America

Table of Contents

Obsessive Compulsive Anonymous

Acknowledgment

We would like to thank Alcoholics Anonymous (A.A.) for allowing us to adapt their Twelve Steps and Twelve Traditions for Obsessive Compulsive Disorders. Their help and cooperation from the start has made our road smoother.

This time-tested program, detailed in "*Alcoholics Anonymous*"[1] and "*Twelve Steps and Twelve Traditions*"[2] has brought recovery for thousands of alcoholics. Patterning Obsessive Compulsive Anonymous after A.A has also brought recovery among us. What follows is Obsessive Compulsive Anonymous' experiences with the Twelve Step program and not those of A.A.

Our personal stories are included in the hope that those reading them might benefit as much as we who have written them.

---

[1]*Alcoholics Anonymous* (New York: A.A. World Services Inc., 1976).
[2]*Twelve Steps and Twelve Traditions* (New York: A.A. World Services Inc., 1981).

Obsessive Compulsive Anonymous

Foreword

Obsessive Compulsive Anonymous (OCA) is a fellowship of people who share their experience, strength and hope with each other that they may solve their common problem and help others to recover from Obsessive Compulsive Disorder (OCD). The only requirement for membership is a desire to recover from OCD. There are no dues or fees; we are self-supporting through our own contributions. OCA is not allied with any sect, denomination, politics, organization or institution; does not wish to engage in any controversy, neither endorses nor opposes any causes. Our primary purpose is to recover from OCD and to help others.*

We choose to remain anonymous at the public level for several good reasons. Anonymity allows us to share our personal stories, knowing that they will remain in the confidence of those who attend our meetings. Anonymity also reinforces that it is the program, not the individual, that is responsible for the recovery.

We hope that by publishing a book of this kind others with OCD will read it and conclude that OCA can also work for them. The recovery program, clearly explained in the following pages, when incorporated into our lives, produces the desired changes which substantially relieves our obsessive-compulsiveness.

If you are alone you may feel afraid that you really can't do this – that it is too much to ask. Remember that it takes only this book and two people with OCD to have a meeting. We have found each other through many avenues and in time you will find others who want this program. We are no longer alone.

---

*The Preamble adapted with permission of the A.A. Grapevine Inc.

Obsessive Compulsive Anonymous

What is Obsessive Compulsive Disorder?

Here we provide the current Diagnostic and Statistical Manual of Mental Disorders, Fourth Edition, description of OCD. We hope the reader will get a general idea of what our symptoms appear to be. If the following description does not seem to fit you-don't be concerned. Perhaps the remainder of the text will strike some familiar chords. All are welcome at our meetings if they think they may belong.

■ **Diagnostic criteria for 300.3 Obsessive-Compulsive Disorder**

A. Either obsessions or compulsions:

Obsessions as defined by (1), (2), (3), and (4):

(1) recurrent and persistent thoughts, impulses, or images that are experienced, at some time during the disturbance, as intrusive and inappropriate and that cause marked anxiety or distress

(2) the thoughts, impulses, or images are not simply excessive worries about real-life problems

(3) the person attempts to ignore or suppress such thoughts, impulses, or images, or to neutralize them with some other thought or action

(4) the person recognizes that the obsessional thoughts, impulses, or images are a product of his or her own mind (not imposed from without as in thought insertion)

Compulsions as defined by (1), and (2):

(1) repetitive behaviors (e.g., hand washing, ordering, checking) or mental acts (e.g., praying, counting, repeating words silently) that the person feels driven to perform in response to an obsession, or according to rules that must be applied rigidly

(2) the behaviors or mental acts are aimed at preventing or reducing distress or preventing some dreaded event or situation; however, these behaviors or mental acts either are not connected in a realistic way with what they are designed to neutralize or prevent or are clearly excessive.

B. At some point during the course of the disorder, the person has recognized that the obsessions or compulsions are excessive or unreasonable. **Note:** This does not apply to children.

C. The obsessions or compulsions cause marked distress, are time consuming (take more than 1 hour a day), or significantly interfere with the person's normal routine, occupational (or academic) functioning, or usual social activities or relationships.

D. If another Axis I disorder is present, the content of the obsessions or compulsions is not restricted to it (e.g. preoccupation with food in the presence of an Eating Disorder; hair pulling in the presence of Trichotillomania; concern with appearance in the presence of Body Dysmorphic Disorder; preoccupation with drugs in the presence of a Substance Use Disorder; preoccupation with having a serious illness in the presence of Hypochondriasis; preoccupation with sexual urges or fantasies in the presence of a Paraphilia; or guilty ruminations in the presence of Major Depressive Disorder).

E. The disturbance is not due to the direct physiological effects of a substance (e.g., a drug of abuse, a medication) or a general medical condition.

Specify if:

With Poor Insight: if, for most of the time during the current episode, the person does not recognize that the obsessions and compulsions are excessive or unreasonable.

Reprinted with permission from the Diagnostic and Statistical Manual of Mental Disorders, Fourth Edition. Copyright 1994 American Psychiatric Association.

To Those of Us Who Are "New" to Obsessive Compulsive Disorder

It seems that OCD has received much attention of late. The last years of the twentieth century have provided an explosion of information about our problem. For some of us, finally accepting that *this* was our problem was a source of comfort after years of confusion.

Unfortunately, many of us were led to believe that we were somehow responsible for getting OCD or that if we weren't so "weak" we would be better already. At OCA we were told that we were not responsible for getting OCD, but that we were responsible for working toward our recovery.

At this writing, the medical and psychological communities appear to have effective treatments for OCD–including medications and behavior therapy–OCA does not endorse any specific treatments for OCD, but *we do recommend that our members see a doctor skilled in the diagnosis and treatment of OCD.* Resources (see the list on the last page of this book) can be contacted for referrals to a professional in your area. OCA is *not* a referral center nor a psychological counseling service.

OCA *is* a fellowship of people who are using the Twelve-Step program to obtain relief from our obsessions and compulsions. We have found that by incorporating the suggestions in this book into our lives we are granted significant relief from our OCD. Those of us at OCA who are receiving professional help for OCD have found this program a welcome addition.

The following are endorsements from professionals who feel that what OCA has to offer can prove beneficial to the OCD sufferer.

Twelve Step Programs and Obsessive Compulsive Disorder: A Note to Mental Health Professionals

Watching a person struggling with Obsessive Compulsive Disorder (OCD) is something like watching an alcoholic trying to fight his disease. In each case, the person may go through alternating phases of the struggle – sometimes trying to fight, control or defeat the compulsion through will power, and at other times denying to himself that any problem exists, even though he might be suffering from serious problems in regard to self-esteem, guilt, interpersonal relationships, and job functioning caused by the disorder. Another similarity between the two disorders is that both are very difficult to treat and some people with these problems have tried many different treatments with little improvement.

The twelve-step program of Alcoholics Anonymous has helped many alcoholics to recover from their disease and to achieve sobriety. The twelve steps have also been used by other self-help groups for various compulsive and addictive problems, including compulsive eating and compulsive gambling. Recently, a new self-help group, Obsessive Compulsive Anonymous (OCA), has started using the twelve steps to help people with OCD. Although it is too early to evaluate the effectiveness of this program, as of this writing (January, 1989), several people in my area have already been helped to greatly reduce their symptoms.

I do not see OCA as a competitor of psychotherapy, behavior therapy, or medication. Rather, I believe that an eclectic, pragmatic, empirical approach to the treatment of OCD can include each of these treatments. One combination of techniques may work better with one individual, while another combination may work more effectively with a different person. For some people, a self-help group such as OCA may be very useful either by itself or in conjunction with psychotherapy, behavior therapy, and/or medication. Research and additional clinical experience will be needed to specify more clearly which approaches work best for which individuals.

For mental health professionals who are unclear as to how or why the twelve-step groups help people, Gregory Bateson (1972)[3] and Robert Arnold (1977)[4] have written articles that analyze the psychological mechanisms through which these programs work. These mechanisms include group support, empathy and concern, specific cognitive techniques to reduce anger and anxiety, identification with people who are successfully recovering from the problem, a spiritual awakening or rebirth, acceptance of the reality of the problem and acceptance of other aspects of reality that were previously denied, restructuring of the individual's personality and character defenses, development of ego strength, an improvement in self-image, improvement in interpersonal relationships, gaining the ability to trust other people, giving up the need to control and manipulate other people, accepting responsibility for one's own life, and overcoming feelings of shame and worthlessness.

[3] Bateson, G. (1972). Steps to an Ecology of the Mind. New York: Ballantine.
[4] Arnold, R.J. (1977). A.A.'s 12 steps as a guide to "ego integrity." Journal of Contemporary Psychotherapy, 9. 62-77.

While mental health professionals working with OCD patients may not accept every aspect of the twelve-step programs, there is no inherent incompatibility between a self-help program based on the steps and most psychotherapeutic approaches. At this point in time, I would suggest an objective attitude on the part of the professionals toward OCA and the twelve steps, as clinical experience begins to accumulate.

By Douglas R. Hogan, Ph.D.,
Clinical Psychologist,
Garden City, New York

Diseases and symptoms aren't really the problem. They're actually the body-mind's attempt to solve a problem – a message from the subconscious to the conscious.

Many traditional medical practitioners are concerned with chipping away at surface needs, merely treating and eliminating the evidence of disease. And, while this is important, it's not enough! The real source for disease lies buried deep beneath the surface.

Real, permanent recovery takes place in the program Obsessive Compulsive Anonymous. OCA encompasses a process of awareness, education and growth, utilizing the twelve step model of Alcoholics Anonymous. It works!

Recovery is never a static state. There are many degrees to the process of recovery, just as there are degrees of illness. Recovery is more than the mere absence of symptoms.

Obsessive Compulsive Anonymous offers hope to the suffering, giving a sense of identification and a knowledge that you aren't alone anymore! Members share their experience, strength and hope through living testimonials. The sense of belonging plus acceptance that members experience becomes the first step *out* of their disease.

Obsessive-compulsives attempt to control their lives by setting excessive routines and rituals that lead to predictable experiences. It's like the unhappy marriage that I describe as "comfortable misery" – so predictable and less threatening.

Many obsessive-compulsives were raised in unpredictable home environments or are currently involved in relationships full of unpredictability. They are able to plan, follow through, and predict how they'll feel after each ritualistic episode.

It's the routineness and reliability of the ritual that is important. But the avoidance of spontaneous feelings impedes

3

the development of intimate relationships and it becomes a disease of *isolation* similar to other addictions.

OCA becomes the process of recovery. It enables members to handle the stress and emotions of everyday life. Healing takes place through a physical, emotional, and spiritual solution which empowers its members with a personal strength beyond explanation.

The twelve steps of recovery, within a non-judgmental fellowship, enable OCA members to live in the "now," one day at a time, knowing they don't have to be perfect. Members feel a definite lessening of restrictions and rules, and learn to trust themselves and others.

That chain of one obsessive-compulsive helping another is spiritual in itself and, in my opinion, provides the essential component for this aspiring fellowship. To quote a phrase of A.A., "It's the love of the fellowship that gets you sober; and it's the 12 steps that keeps you sober."

Obsessive Compulsive Anonymous creates the pathway to serenity. Self-responsibility and love are the foundations in the pursuit of balance and integrity.

Janet Greeson, Ph.D.
Your Life Matters, A consulting service for matters of the Heart.
800-515-1995

North Raleigh Psychiatry &
Addiction Medicine, P.A.
920-A Paverstone Drive
Raleigh, North Carolina 27615

March 12, 1990

Obsessive Compulsive Anonymous
P.O. Box 215
New Hyde Park, NY 11040

Dear Fellowship of OCA:

I want to thank you for your kindness in sending me the draft of the Obsessive Compulsive Anonymous organization manual.

I read it with considerable interest and want to congratulate you and your colleagues for the creation of the very excellent publication. I have been referring my patients with OCD to a 12 Step Recovery Program for some 6 years. I feel that a spiritual program structured by the 12 Steps is a realistic adaptation to any chronic illness. I send my best wishes for every success in achieving publication of your "Big Book."

With kindest regards, I remain

Sincerely yours,

Wilmer C. Betts, M.D.
WCB/gfb

Thomas E. Lauer, M.D., Diplomate in Psychiatry
High Point Medical Center
624 Quaker Lane, Suite A-111
High Point, North Carolina 27262

February 19, 1990

Obsessive Compulsive Anonymous
Post Office Box 215
New Hyde Park, NY 11040

Dear Fellowship of OCA:

It has been my experience in working with individuals who are in recovery from chemical dependency to recognize that the addiction model shares much with obsessive compulsive disorder. Specifically, we see in alcoholics the mental obsession to drink, followed by the first drink, and the subsequent onset of compulsive drinking. This tends to be even more significantly seen in the use of other potent mood altering chemicals such as Heroin and Cocaine. Indeed we even recognize that in certain affective disorders, e.g., manic depressive illness, that the onset of a manic episode produces a pleasurable stimulus for the individual, a resulting desire to continue with that pleasurable stimulus, and indeed an escalation into full blown mania, this being quite out of control.

It is also true from my experience, that the individual with obsessive compulsive disorder becomes involved in certain obsessions, finding their ultimate relief only in carrying out their ritualistic compulsive behaviors.

For those of us familiar with the spiritual aspects of mental health it is quite clear that many individuals will respond very positively to a 12 step recovery program. This is particularly true if a person can become honest, open minded, and willing to change. The ultimate surrender of the individual with obsessive compulsive disorder, and the involvement in a spiritual program of recovery will be successful in virtually every case for those who persevere.

I strongly endorse the program of Obsessive Compulsive Anonymous for anyone who is seeking recovery from their obsessive compulsive disorder.

Yours sincerely,

Thomas E. Lauer, M.D.

TEL/bh

Spirituality for a Twelve Step Program for Compulsive and Obsessive Behavior

by Father Leo Booth

It is often said, and said with enthusiasm, that the key to recovery from addiction, compulsive and obsessive behavior, is spirituality. Most treatment centers and therapy agencies are concerned to stress spirituality as an important aspect of recovery. All Twelve Step programs are spiritual, basing themselves on the "spiritual awakening" that enables continual recovery as a daily basis.

But what is spirituality? For many people (although not everyone) it is easier to spell than explain. Indeed spirituality is often a cause of anger and debate, often confused with religion. Obsessive-compulsives are sometimes reluctant to embrace a program that might be considered suspiciously religious in nature – especially if they or their parents have suffered ridicule, condemnation and ostracization at the hands of ministers, priests or rabbis. I would like to suggest that this "key to recovery," this important aspect of wellness is often the source of confusion, not least amongst professionals: perhaps for this reason spirituality is mentioned and emphasized rather than explained!

In this article I shall seek to explain spirituality and apply it to the treatment and on-going recovery programs for compulsive and obsessive people. In my book "Spirituality and Recovery: A Guide to Positive Living," I defined spirituality as being that God-given ingredient (given to *all* human beings, regardless of color, culture or creed) that enables the development of a positive and creative lifestyle. Spirituality is the activated outcome of being made in the image of God. Spirituality reminds us that we were created to create. Therein lies our responsibility. My understanding of spirituality is not simply seen in placing our future dependency upon a Higher Power, but rather stresses an understanding of spirituality more as a precious gift from God that requires nurturing and nourishment. We are responsible for the development of spirituality in our lives.

Spirituality is also not just concerned with prayer and meditation, although I understand that we can give a broad definition of both these topics. Spirituality is concerned with the WHOLE human being; that involves the body, mind and emotions. If it really is true that God does not make junk then this comprehensive approach to spirituality makes incredible sense. It also absorbs all the various aspects of the treatment modality and recovery agencies into its catchment: doctors, clergy, nurses, therapists, nutritionists, physiotherapists, counselors, sponsors and fellow members of a Twelve Step group. In other words all those who are involved in developing a positive and creative life-style are involved in this dynamic concept of spirituality.

How does this definition help those suffering from a dysfunctional, obsessive and compulsive behavior pattern? Well it clearly reminds the sufferers that they need to be involved in their healing, their recovery. To believe in a miracle is to understand that you *are* that miracle. Spirituality involves developing and maintaining a change in attitude and behavior. Perhaps when Adam and Eve sought an answer to their human problems in the forbidden fruit from the tree (so they could be "as God") obsessive and compulsive behavior was born into the world.

Spirituality confronts "the Lie" that has plagued humankind throughout our history – we cannot find a solution to our problems outside of ourselves. Indeed if we look for solutions outside of ourselves we only create more problems. There is no obsession or compulsion that can take away the pain of being imperfect. There is no controlling behavior pattern or set of beliefs that will ever make us "as God." There is no escape from the moments of suffering that affects every human being at some time in their lives. Seeking such a fix can lead to obsessive-compulsive behavior.

Spirituality reminds us that we are *all* children of God. The compelling message in the first chapters of Genesis is important to hear today: *What God made is good.* Guilt, shame, judgments and self-pity are the tools that compulsive and obsessive behavior uses to beat us into slavery. And it seems to be working. To believe "The Lie" that human beings have no merit or divine power in their own right is to eventually live that lie.

I am reminded of a story that carries a warning, especially for the religious amongst us. A man visited a town where on every cross street was a church or mission hall. "My word," the stranger said, "These people must surely love God." "I truly hope so," said an old lady in a local shop, "because they sure do a good job of hating each other!"

We are all children of God. We have the spiritual power to create loving lives. The responsibility for recovery from compulsive and obsessive behavior is ours. God's miracle exists within each of us.

Father Leo Booth
1 (800) 284-2804

Western Suffolk Psychological Services
755 New York Avenue – Suite 200
Huntington, New York 11743

These days, no one questions the value of support and self-help groups. Knowing that you are not alone, getting validation for what you are going through, being able to talk to someone who understands exactly what you are saying, and finding out what does or doesn't help your problem are what most people seek in such meetings. Having been a close outside observer of Obsessive Compulsive Anonymous (OCA) since its beginnings, I can say that not only does it provide its members with these things, it also does a lot more.

I believe that while everyone has a philosophy of life (whether they realize it or not), some philosophies are better than others. Furthermore, a good philosophy helps you to cope with the inevitable problems and hardships you will encounter in life. Not having one is like entering the jungle without survival training. To my way of thinking, a good support group provides it members with the opportunity to develop a good workable philosophy. This is exactly what OCA does. The Serenity Prayer, alone, which is the cornerstone of all 12-step groups says more as a philosophy of life in just a few words than many lengthy volumes I have read.

Over the years I have had the opportunity to treat a large number of individuals with OCD, some of whom were OCA members. My observation has been that those who took what the group had to offer had more patient, positive attitudes, and were better able to take the trials of getting recovered in stride. I have watched OCA grow from a single local support group to a regional network of neighboring meetings. I am pleased that my patients have such places to go, where they will get help, support, and the encouragement to think straighter about how to help themselves out of the corner their disorder has pushed them into. I only wish that sufferers everywhere had access to these meetings.

Does OCA help everyone? The answer is no. However, nothing helps everyone. To think otherwise is naive. Can meetings make you better? Again, the answer is no. Meetings represent opportunities, and can only help you if you, yourself, make the effort to use what they are giving you. For those who are open to the OCA message, and who show a willingness to put it to work in their lives each day, it can be a lifesaver, filling in many of the blank places on the roadmap they will need to help them find the way back. So to OCA I say, "Keep up the good work, and keep doing it one day at a time!"

Fred Penzel, Ph.D.
Psychologist

What We Have Discovered at OCA

We, as a fellowship, have found that together we can get well when separately we could not. Many of us have spent countless hours "battling" our obsessions and compulsions, swearing them off forever only to find ourselves right back where we started. *There is a solution!* The Twelve Steps, as originated by Alcoholics Anonymous, and adapted for OCD, can bring much relief to our common dilemma. Most of us have found that using this program together in the meetings can reduce or eliminate our obsessions and compulsions. We have found it most helpful in our meetings to emphasize the Twelve Steps and the program literature while discussing our personal stories, since it is the program that brings the much-desired relief. Discussions of a personal nature are encouraged, but are used to reinforce how we apply the program in our lives today.

We have also found it useful to emphasize how we practice the program today. Examples include calling our sponsors, helping other people with OCD, taking our inventories and praying to a Higher Power (to be discussed in the chapter "The Recovery Program.") We have found this daily emphasis much more satisfying than dwelling on our obsessions and compulsions and whether we had a "good or bad" day with them. If we practice the program on a daily basis, our obsessions and compulsions will take on less importance and our program will take root to grow and flourish, providing us relief.

It appears that meetings can provide a daily foundation for our recovery because it is there that we are reminded of who we are and what the program suggests we do to recover. There are a whole host of anonymous Twelve Step groups which welcome us with open arms. We suggest you call your local self-help clearinghouse to find out what program is available in your area if OCA is not nearby. Although these other Twelve Step meetings may not specifically address OCD, you can still find the program and the fellowship, and take this applied knowledge in starting a local OCA group. This will often reinforce your recovery even further.

Lastly, if you are not familiar with what you find in this book, relax; you do not have to understand or apply it all at once. Gradually much of what is discussed here will begin to infiltrate your life and the desired changes will come. In the meantime, read on and attend meetings.

The Recovery Program

Our program of recovery is one that works. Here you will find the "Twelve Steps" which have been our key to a new life. Many of you will feel that this is too much to ask, that it won't work for you. We only ask that you give it a fraction of the time and energy you've put into perpetuating your OCD.

As we began to follow these suggestions our lives improved and our OCD lessened. Since ours is a program of action, actually *doing* what is outlined here seems to produce the results. With God's help we move away from our obsessive-compulsiveness and into a fellowship of recovering friends.

Here are the steps that outline our program:

Step 1. We admitted we were powerless over our obsessions and compulsions – that our lives had become unmanageable.

Step 2. Came to believe that a Power greater than ourselves could restore us to sanity.

Step 3. Made a decision to turn our will and our lives over to the care of God *as we understood Him.*

Step 4. Made a searching and fearless moral inventory of ourselves.

Step 5. Admitted to God, to ourselves, and to another human being the exact nature of our wrongs.

Step 6. Were entirely ready to have God remove all these defects of character.

Step 7. Humbly asked Him to remove our shortcomings.

Step 8. Made a list of all persons we had harmed, and became willing to make amends to them all.

Step 9. Made direct amends to such people wherever possible, except when to do so would injure them or others.

Step 10. Continued to take personal inventory and when we were wrong promptly admitted it.

Step 11. Sought through prayer and meditation to improve our conscious contact with God *as we understood Him,* praying only for knowledge of His will for us and the power to carry that out.

Step 12. Having had a spiritual awakening as the result of these steps, we tried to carry this message to those who still suffer from Obsessive Compulsive Disorder, and to practice these principles in all our affairs.*

The 12 Steps of A.A.

1. We admitted we were powerless over alcohol - that our lives had become unmanageable.

2. Came to believe that a Power greater than ourselves could restore us to sanity.

3. Made a decision to turn our will and our lives over to the care of God, AS WE UNDERSTOOD HIM.

4. Made a searching and fearless moral inventory of ourselves.

5. Admitted to God, to ourselves and to another human being the exact nature of our wrongs.

6. Were entirely ready to have God remove all these defects of character.

7. Humbly asked Him to remove our shortcomings.

8. Made a list of all persons we had harmed, and became willing to make amends to them all.

---

*A.A.'s Twelve Steps adapted with permission of A.A. World Services Inc.

9. Made direct amends to such people wherever possible, except when to do so would injure them or others.

10. Continued to take personal inventory and when we were wrong promptly admitted it.

11. Sought through prayer and meditation to improve our conscious contact with God AS WE UNDERSTOOD HIM, praying only for knowledge of His will for us and the power to carry that out.

12. Having had a spiritual awakening as the result of these steps, we tried to carry this message to alcoholics, and to practice these principles in all our affairs.

The Twelve Steps are reprinted and adapted with permission of Alcoholics Anonymous World Services Inc. Permission to reprint and adapt this material does not mean that A.A. has reviewed or approved the contents of this publication, nor that A.A. agrees with the views expressed herein. A.A. is a program of recovery from alcoholism *only* – use of the Twelve Steps in connection with programs and activities that are patterned after A.A., but which address other problems, does not imply otherwise.

.

Step 1. *We admitted we were powerless over our obsessions and compulsions – that our lives had become unmanageable.* Obsessive Compulsive Disorder had us "licked." The more we wrestled with our illness, the harder it fought back. It is only by admitting we were losing our lone battles against OCD that we could recover to enjoy happy and fulfilling lives.

When first presented with this concept, most of us were surprised. We came to OCA expecting to build up will power against OCD. Instead we learned we were victims of obsessions and compulsions so strong that unaided will power didn't work. Almost every time we got into the trenches with our OCD we emerged the losers. In OCA we surrendered to the reality that completing rituals and dwelling on obsessions never worked for us in the end. Acceptance, on a gut level, that we cannot "negotiate" with our obsessions and compulsions is our admission of powerlessness.

Many of us could not admit that our lives had become unmanageable since we might still have had good jobs, our families or nice homes. We were then told that unmanageability doesn't mean that we had to lose these things, although others of us did. The first step says that our lives had become unmanageable, and for some of us, not being able to enjoy our lives was unmanageable enough.

When we became ready to do *anything* to lift this merciless problem from ourselves, we were ready for the rest of the program.

Step 2. *Came to believe that a Power greater than ourselves could restore us to sanity.* This step asks us to believe in something which many of us feel we cannot. Some of us won't believe in a Higher Power, others can't. Still others who do believe in something have no faith whatsoever that a miracle will be performed on their behalf. Others felt that belief in a Higher Power was totally unscientific and just nonsense.

It appears that the *belief* in a power that could restore us to sanity is all that is needed. Many recovering from Obsessive Compulsive Disorders maintain that since they made an attempt to believe in a Higher Power they got results. The minute we stopped arguing and fighting this point, Step 2 gradually came to us.

To effect this approach, some of us have made our groups the "Higher Power'" since they are certainly a power greater than just one lone individual suffering with OCD.

Those who lack faith often feel that God has turned His back on them. Organized religion was just another corporate enterprise; besides, prayer never helped anyway.

The answer has to do with the quality of faith rather than its quantity. The fact is we never applied the 12 Steps to clean up our side of the road so that the Grace of God could relieve our obsessions and compulsions. We never acknowledged our personality defects, made amends to those we hurt (including ourselves), or unselfishly tried to help another with OCD.

Whether agnostic, atheist, or believer, we can take the second step to the best of our ability right here and now.

Step 3. *Made a decision to turn our will and our lives over to the care of God as we understood Him.* At first glance Step 3 seemed impossible to many of us. Fortunately we can tell you that by just coming to a meeting or reading this book you have already begun this important step. All who have joined OCA and intend to try, have already begun to set aside their self-will to listen to another's ideas about Obsessive Compulsive Disorder.

The facts speak for themselves – the more we work for the willingness to depend upon a Power greater than ourselves the more independent and happy we become. Obviously our problems haven't been solved by will power since "playing God" hasn't worked well for us.

People with OCD are fortunate in the sense that we have suffered enough under our own rigid guidelines for life that we were driven to this program which allows us to look to a different source for guidance. Often we are victimized by remorse and guilt when we think of how OCD has affected our lives. Our lone courage and unaided will cannot bring us out of our lonely OCD prison.

Step 3 must be given a fair try since many of our troubles have been caused by the misuse of will power.

We have tried to bombard our problems with it instead of attempting to bring it into agreement with God's intention for us.[5] Our self-centered obsessive thoughts and compulsive behaviors have left us little room for those we care about. We could not change this frame of mind by wishing or trying on our own power. We had to have God's help.

The decision to turn our will and our lives over to the care of a Higher Power must be given a determined and persistent effort. Some of us have turned our will over in stages, maybe at first to the program and group of people in the program. We look for our Higher Power to express himself through others since God often works through people. This can often develop into the willingness to depend upon a Higher Power who is "running the show" for us. Acceptance of God's will for us leaves us free to enjoy life instead of fighting it all the time. We are no longer in "control" - we live life on life's terms. We still exert ourselves, though, applying the principles of this program to grow into our new way of life.

The Serenity Prayer can be used at any time we feel that we are losing our "God consciousness." We simply say, "God grant me the serenity to accept the things I cannot change, courage to change the things I can and the wisdom to know the difference." We reaffirm here that God's will, not ours, will be done.

Step 4. *Made a searching and fearless moral inventory of ourselves.* An inventory of our liabilities now will free up our lives later. Many of us did not realize that we were carrying so much "emotional baggage" until we thoroughly did this step. Some of us also felt that we really were defect-free except for our obsessive and compulsive behaviors. Still others said that their present anxieties and troubles were caused by the behavior of other people who should change their ways.

[5]*Twelve Steps and Twelve Traditions* (New York A.A. World Services Inc. 1981), p.40.

Step 4 is a comprehensive effort to reveal the defects of character that are hurting ourselves and others. We clean up only *our* side of the road and do not look for the wrongs done by others.

Many of us have felt that a written list of resentments was a good place to start since resentments hurt us more than we know.

A suggested approach:

I'm resentful at.	The Cause	Affects my:
(People, Institutions, or principles)	(Why we were angry)	
Mr. Doe	Unreasonable boss Doesn't appreciate my abilities	May lose job Self-esteem (fear)
Myself	Obsessive compulsive behavior	Self-esteem (fear)
My spouse	Opinionated Domineering	Pride Sex relations

This list of resentments and their effects allows us to crystallize their impact on our lives.

Others have found their defects in the "seven deadly sins" of pride, greed, lust, anger, gluttony, envy and sloth. Those full of pride often feel that they don't need to look any further, that all their problems are caused by factors outside themselves. Others may feel that they have a right to be angry since the world hasn't been kind to them and people have wronged them. Some still believe they have to grab more of everything and when disappointed, take their frustrations out on others. The simple fact for us is that holding on to these defects of character makes us sick. This is also true if we were justified in these feelings. Anger and resentment shut us out from spiritual growth and move us back into our destructive patterns. We simply cannot afford to harbor these feelings if we want to recover.

Fear often touches every aspect of our lives. Many of us found ourselves in an environment where fear was the daily norm. Physical, sexual or emotional abuse were obvious sources of our constant fears. Others of us grew up in environments where the "fear of life" was taught early on. We were led to believe that the world was an entirely dangerous place and that we had to watch our every move. By reviewing our fears thoroughly and putting them on paper we expose them for what they are. We use the same chart as we did for our resentments, listing also the causes and effects of our fears. We meet those fears with faith once we look to a Higher Power and the fellowship for guidance.

Sex is sometimes very troublesome but can be dealt with as any other life situation. We look for anger, resentments, jealousy and envy and ask for guidance. We list those whom we hurt with our sex conduct, what we did, and how it ultimately affected us. We also must not forget those times we used sex as a weapon, perhaps by withholding it from our mates or flirting outside our relationship. We often find that honestly asking ourselves, "Did I act selfishly?" can serve as a guiding direction.

We often end our inventory by looking at our relationships with family and friends. Here we find ourselves dominating these people, or to the other extreme, leaning on them too heavily. This self-centered behavior can only add to our problems. We must form partnerships with people, and look at how we can help others rather than at what they should be doing for us.

We hope that the reader will examine this step closely since our defects are often buried under layers of self-justification. We take this step to the best of our ability, now knowing that this is the beginning of a lifelong process with Step 10.

Step 5. *Admitted to God, to ourselves, and to another human being the exact nature of our wrongs.* Here we are given the opportunity to dump all the garbage we have been carrying around since it is this load that increases our obsessive-compulsive behavior. We know from a personal vantage point that we tended to be secretive about our OCD because we felt it was embarrassing, personal, or that people just wouldn't understand. But upon closer inspection we sometimes found that we kept this problem a secret because we didn't want any-one to interfere with our little rituals or obsessions; *we simply would deal with them on our own.* Here in Step 5 we find that opening communication with God and another human being lifts this burden of secrecy from us. We soon get used to the idea that God knows all about us after all.

But it is when we are honest with another person that it confirms we have been honest with ourselves and with God. We share our inventory with someone whose only real job is to listen and offer advice as needed. Here we turn back to Step 4 where we focused in on our defects of character. We experi-ence humility by confiding these defects with a trusted individual. This may be another member of the group, a close friend, therapist, clergyperson or sponsor. We also learn where we might have exaggerated or dramatized our shortcomings. We find where our stock-taking has been productive, and learn from this "housecleaning."

At this point many of us have experienced great relief by emerging from the isolation our obsessive-compulsiveness has imposed on us. Our burden of guilt and shame is no longer ours to bear alone. The focus begins to move away from our personal concerns into the stream of life once we let God and someone else into our world.

Step 6. *Were entirely ready to have God remove all these defects of character.* This step appears to be something we would like to do. Who would want to hang on to his defects of character? But experience shows that most of us are only willing to let go of some of these defects while holding on tightly to others. We are perhaps "comfortable" with some of our old attitudes and ways or maybe we just don't know how we can live without our own rigid guidelines. We can tell you that as God removes our defects of character we are freed from the self-imposed prison that Obsessive Compulsive Disorder wraps us in.

Here we do not expect the immediate removal of our defects. Patient improvement is what we strive for and in God's time much of what is objectionable will be lifted.

Let us examine some of our defects more closely now. Perfectionism is one we seem to see a lot of. By trying to make things "perfect" (which is impossible) we destroy our chances for a happy life. Our repeated attempts to make things "perfect" only bring on anxiety and stress which in turn fuel this fire. We must look to a Higher Power and the program for guidance in this matter since self-knowledge doesn't work. *Acceptance* can replace our perfectionistic tendencies when we "let go" of our control.

Self-righteous anger can be a very dangerous defect of character. We sometimes take satisfaction with anger because of how someone has wronged us. We may blame other people for our problems because of things they said or did. Even if we have a "right" to be angry we cannot stay so for long if we hope for spiritual growth.

Self-pity seems to be a common character defect we share. For some reason we look to "whine" about our state of affairs, feeling sorry for ourselves and crying in our cups. Many of us feel that we have been dealt an unfair hand in the game of life and if only *all* of our OCD and other problems would go away we would be happy. Through our program we come to accept that although things in our lives might be better, we really are *not* bearing the weight of the world. *Everyone* has their own problems and OCD just happens to be ours. We don't believe we were responsible for getting OCD, but now that we have it we need to work a recovery program for it. We have found it helpful when we start to feel sorry for ourselves to put energy instead into helping another member of OCA.

"Control" seems to be a problematic area for most of us. Our obsessive-compulsive nature looks to control our environment and thoughts in a way that is excessive and self-destructive. On the other hand we often find ourselves dominated by other people who "control" us. We instead need to set clear boundaries between others and ourselves so that our personal freedoms and desires can be expressed. By declaring our emotional independence from controlling individuals we are further freed from our obsessive-compulsiveness.

This action may take courage and patience but the end result is change and personal integrity. We no longer fall back on our control games with others - we have the option of leaving any personal rut we find ourselves in. We need no longer be trapped in controlling families, jobs or relations. Action and change go hand in hand with our recovery from OCD.

Another defect of character we seem to share involves our *inability to change* the things that are clearly hurting us. A prime example is seen in our self-destructive relationships with certain people. These relationships may be found in our jobs, families and friendships. As we work our program of recovery we look for guidance concerning these personal matters. *We*

29

don't have to stay with people who pull us down into our obsessive-compulsive ways. We look for the courage to sever these relationships – which we originally thought we couldn't function without. Of course there will be situations in which repairing the relationship is also an option-but we must be ready to put our recovery from OCD first. This may mean making a swift, clean break from a truly destructive dependency on another, no matter how painful that may be.

Another common trait among us has been called "terminal uniqueness." Somehow we believed our problems were different from almost everyone else's, and our types of OCD symptoms just *had* to be the worst. Many of us also share the defect of blaming our variation of Obsessive Compulsive Disorder (and ourselves) for the situations we have gotten into. This is really just pride and ego in reverse (or negative) pride. It seems that we either build ourselves up to heights which we cannot attain or cut ourselves down by assassination of our "uniquely bad" characters. In OCA we learn that OCD is just OCD and that our "brand" of symptoms really isn't so special after all. *Acceptance of ourselves where we are right NOW puts us on the road to recovery.*

Procrastination seems to be another defect we share. In an effort to plan things out "just right" we end up planning and not doing. Recovery from OCD often lies in our feet – not our heads. We need to take positive actions in order to get positive results. We have found that by "living in the now" we can take more timely action.

Having overly high expectations of ourselves and others is another character trait that hurts our recovery. It seems we often demand more than is humanly possible from ourselves and others. By setting more realistic goals for ourselves and lightening up on our expectations for others we further our recovery. Also, when it comes to *our own* recoveries, we are usually the least patient of all. In OCA we have found recovery to be a process, not an event. When we open ourselves to the healing and allow the changes to happen we *do* get better!

This program allows us to progress toward the goal of readiness to part with our defects of character. We continue to work with this objective in Step 7, moving towards God's will for us.

Step 7. *Humbly asked Him to remove our shortcomings.* Without humility our chances of recovery are greatly lessened. We saw earlier that we were indeed powerless over our obsessions and compulsions and that a power greater than ourselves could restore us to sanity. It was by admitting defeat and turning to a strength outside ourselves that we were able to initiate recovery. Here in this step we begin to become convinced that living on our own individual strength and intelligence alone makes a working faith in a Higher Power impossible.

It appears that the chief activator of our obsessive-compulsiveness has been self-centered fear – primarily fear that we would lose something we already possessed or would fail to get something we demanded. Living upon a basis of unsatisfied demands we were in a state of continual disturbance and frustration.[6] We were constantly demanding things to be just the way we wanted them to be instead of aligning our will with that of God's.

It seems among us that we've often placed material achievements and external comforts above character building and spiritual values. We do not wish to minimize material achievement and success, but we can tell you from experience that living solely along these lines drives us back into our obsessive-compulsiveness. With humility as our guide, we move away from these "externals" in our world toward helping our fellow man and improving our relationship with our

[6] *Twelve Steps and Twelve Traditions* (New York: A.A. World Services, Inc. 1981). p.76.

Higher Power.

For us this new outlook comes only after repeated sufferings with our own self-destructive attitudes and behaviors. In our fellowship we have seen how the misery of OCD is transformed by humility into something positive. We hear story after story of how humility has brought *strength* out of weakness. Our character defects have led us into making unreasonable demands upon ourselves, others and God. We are now willing to apply humility toward removing our shortcomings so that we may be of better service to those around us. Most of us have found that our shortcomings which fire our obsessive-compulsiveness are gradually removed in God's time.

Step 8. *Made a list of all persons we had harmed, and became willing to make amends to them all.* Here we look for the willingness to face those we have hurt, and the means to best repair the damage done. We have actually made a beginning with our moral inventory in Step 4. We turn to our charts of resentment, fear and sex conduct to find the people we have harmed.

When looking at a troubled relationship, we often go on the defensive. We may only want to look at how we have been hurt instead of at the total picture. Often we have strained the relationship to bring out the worst in others. Some of us, still troubled with denial, cling to the proposition that our OCD never hurt anybody but ourselves. Certainly we hurt ourselves, but we must not forget the suffering we inflicted on those we cared for the most. They *also* were the victims of our obsessions and compulsions. We do not wish to enter into a debate over whether we were responsible for the suffering our illness inflicted, but we do know that we hurt others and to recover we must be willing to make amends.

Many of us have found that our obsessive-compulsiveness

has harmed others on levels previously unexplored. Some subtler ways we have emotionally and spiritually hurt people may be seen in our family lives. We may happen to be inflexible, callous, critical, impatient or humorless; we may wallow in self-pity or lash out at others. We can also bring these attitudes into our day-to-day affairs, making life harder for all around us. We now use this new-found outlook to find those people who have been negatively affected-meanwhile forgiving the wrongs done to us. We are looking for the willingness to forgive ourselves and others for the rough spots in our personal relationships. The willingness to make amends can free us from our resentments, which ultimately frees us from our obsessive-compulsiveness.

There might be some instances where restitution is impossible. Examples include people who have died, those who won't agree to talk with us, or amends better deferred for other reasons. This doesn't excuse us from an accurate survey of our past life as it has affected other people. In taking this step we should avoid extreme judgments of both ourselves and others and be most careful not to exaggerate our task at hand.

Step 9. *Made direct amends to such people wherever possible, except when to do so would injure them or others.* In this step, we find our sea of resentments "washing clean." It is here that we meet with those on our list and attempt to repair the damage done, freeing us into "emotional sobriety."

The people we make amends to will often be receptive to our approach, even if we hurt them beyond repair. But it seems we often find that many of our conflicts have been one sided with only us holding onto anger. We seem to be of the temperament to hold a grudge long beyond the average fellow's forgetting of the same. Here we are allowed to forgive both others and ourselves for those stored emotions which have hurt us so.

There will also be certain amends which are not so benign. Obviously, if we have cheated someone in some way, we should rectify the problem as soon as possible. Our self-centeredness can easily compromise our natural tendencies to be honest and fair. It is most important in the amends process that we do not *increase* the harm we have already done. Examples include revealing names in a detailed account of an extra-marital affair when your spouse suspects nothing. Or perhaps we have padded an expense account which our associates little suspect. Here we must look carefully with the guidance of a Higher Power and those in the program to decide how these situations must be handled. What we are trying to do is heal these problems, not throw salt on the wound. We must be certain not to injure others or ourselves further, but we must be willing to make amends as fast and as far as we possibly can.

It seems appropriate here to mention self-forgiving in the amends process. We have often been our own worst enemies regarding our obsessive-compulsiveness. Here we can forgive ourselves and accept that we are OK where we are now.

If we are serious about working on our recovery we will feel amazing results before we are halfway done. We will taste a new freedom from our obsessive-compulsiveness. We will accept our past and grow from it. We will feel peace of mind that we never thought possible. We will realize that our experience can now help others. Self-pity and shame will leave us. Our self-centeredness will be replaced with a trust in others and God. Our negative attitudes and behaviors will decrease. Our insecurities and fears concerning people will lessen. We will now welcome change instead of fear it. Our priorities and concerns will move away from ourselves and into helping others. Self-hate will be replaced with self-esteem. Life will no longer be a constant struggle with no relief in sight. We will feel God working in our lives today.

Are these exaggerated promises? We know they are not. They are happening for us. If we work for them they will always materialize in time.

Step 10. *Continued to take personal inventory and when we were wrong promptly admitted it.* A continuous look at our liabilities (as well as assets) seems to be necessary for us. We need to survey our attitudes during the day, watching for anger, resentment, fear, inflexibility and self-centered thinking. Daily we cast up a balance sheet and semi-annually we go in for a total housecleaning. Many of us felt that these practices were too time consuming and really didn't apply. We found out instead that these few minutes spent in self-examination saved us hours of suffering with our obsessions and compulsions. Making this practice a daily part of our lives makes us happier and allows us to be more kind and tolerant towards others.

A spot-check inventory can be taken during the day anytime we are disturbed by anger, self-pity, resentments or a host of other character defects we have previously identified. In these situations in our lives we need to look for self-restraint and a willingness to admit when the fault is ours. We should avoid speaking or acting hastily which can damage our relationships with others. We must avoid argument and criticism with others, as well as silent anger.

We can try to stop making unreasonable demands upon those we love, including ourselves. We can show unselfishness towards those we've frequently ignored. It will become more and more evident in time that it is senseless to become angry or to get hurt by people who are also living in this sometimes difficult world of ours. In this continuous look at our inventory we strive for progress, not perfection.

When evening comes many of us draw up a balance sheet

for the day. Credit and Debit are present on this paper since we often do constructive things during our day despite our character defects. We look for motives in our thoughts or acts since our motives will determine if we were selfish or not. We sometimes find ourselves hiding a bad intention underneath a veil of good. We needlessly argued with someone because we were full of fear and anger or we complained about our state of affairs seeking only attention and sympathy. "If only people would see it our way," we wailed. This veil of self-righteousness has to be lifted if we hope to change.

Putting this step to daily use with the help of our friends in the program will allow us to spot more quickly the defects of character which drag us down into our obsessive compulsiveness. If we have an honest regret for harms done and a willingness to try for better tomorrows we will grow away from our problems and into God's solution for us.

Step 11. *Sought through prayer and meditation to improve our conscious contact with God as we understood Him, praying only for knowledge of His will for us and the power to carry that out.* Prayer and meditation can work for us even if our beliefs lean toward those of the agnostic or atheist. There is a direct linkage among self-examination, meditation and prayer. Taken separately these practices can bring much relief and benefit. But when they are logically related and interwoven the result is an unshakable foundation for life.[7]

Simply experimenting with prayer and meditation can lead to unexplained results. Some of us have found that by applying the concept of "just for today" we are able to pray today — not committing ourselves to a lifetime of recitals. This approach allows us to resume prayer if we find that this part of our program has fallen by the wayside.

Many of us have found that beginning and ending our days

[7] *Twelve Steps and Twelve Traditions* (New York: A.A. World Services, Inc. 1981), p. 98.

with prayer has given us new strength. We can find many wonderful prayers from an infinite variety of sources. Our sponsors or spiritual advisors can guide us to them. When meditating we listen for direction from our Higher Power, looking for knowledge of His or Her will for us. Upon awakening we can renew our relationship with our Higher Power and our program.

When we pray we must be careful not to ask for specific things because we don't know if what we are praying for is in accord with God's will. We do know that God loves us and wants us to be happy, and that this happiness can be found by aligning our wills with a Higher Power's will. As the day goes on we can pause when situations must be met and renew the simple request, "Thy will, not mine, be done."

A Higher Power may not always answer our prayers in the manner in which we might expect. God speaks through many mediums, of which we may be aware of only a few. We have found that decision-making is more fruitful if we make use of this program and the people in it for guidance and support on any matters we face. We don't *have* to be alone anymore. The world may not seem so hostile now; we are no longer lost, frightened and purposeless. Prayer and meditation have brought a Higher Power into our daily affairs.

Step 12. *Having had a spiritual awakening as the result of these steps, we tried to carry this message to those who still suffer from Obsessive Compulsive Disorder, and to practice these principles in all our affairs.* Here we are given a chance to bring the message of recovery to those who still live in the lonely prison of OCD. This vital step is done enthusiastically without thought of reward or praise. *Our* stage of OCD recovery is unimportant. We can still spread this program even if we are the newest of new or if we have had a relapse.

Here we must also talk about the "spiritual awakening" as a result of taking the previous eleven steps. Thankfully, this doesn't mean we have all experienced a sudden profound uplifting. More often a gradual rearrangement of our attitudes and priorities results in a new state of consciousness which we previously thought impossible. We have plugged ourselves into a source of strength which affords us peace of mind, unselfishness, tolerance and love. We are able to do, feel and believe things which we couldn't on our own.

Since OCD often has isolated us from the rest of the world, the twelfth step brings us out of our self-imposed prison. When carrying this message to others, we interact with people like us who uniquely understand. No longer are our obsessions and compulsions ours to bear alone. We have a fellowship which will come through for us if we are willing to get out of ourselves to help and be helped by others.

When meeting someone who might be interested in our program we have found it best to stick to our own stories. We are not in a position to preach or educate. Our experience is our best advocate. There will be those who might reject this approach citing that it isn't scientific or doesn't apply to them. Don't argue this point, just explain what OCA has done for you. Working with others is the foundation of our recovery. A kind act or an occasional phone call won't cut it. We must let others into our lives in order to recover, lest we go back to our old painful, destructive ways.

We have also found that those of us who are receiving medical or psychological help for their OCD can also work this program with good results. We, as a fellowship, take no position on specific outside treatments. We do know that this program has helped us tremendously.

Practicing these principles in all of our affairs simply

asks us to take our program with us in whatever situation we may find ourselves. Many of us have noticed that if we practice program daily, we find ourselves watching our resentments and anger, forgiving others of their mistakes and in general a greater tolerance and acceptance of life just the way it is. Our demands for the world to be just the way *we* want it to be will lessen. We may start, instead, to think how we can make someone else's day easier instead of how difficult our own lives can be.

Before program, many of us saw our OCD aggravated by situations around us or problems we may have had. So in response, we tried to arrange these situations to our satisfaction, hoping that this change in our external world would help our OCD. Through OCA we came to realize that the changes must instead come from within. We also saw that we had to think of others outside of ourselves, especially those still suffering from OCD. We try to carry the "OCA spirit" into our daily work, our personal relations, and our relationship with our Higher Power. We, who have struggled alone for so long with OCD, have found that in trying to help others, our personal struggles with OCD take on less importance. This is the paradox we have found. The solution lies *outside* of ourselves and rests with the willingness to help and be helped by others and our Higher Power.

Another benefit we have found by bringing program into our day-to-day affairs is the change we have had in our relationship with others. Previously we have found ourselves overly dependent on people as a sick child on his parent or to the other extreme, welcoming no one's help or opinions into our lives, living exclusively by our own rigid guidelines. Often we lived in shame, isolating ourselves from others and thinking that no one could possibly understand. Instead, we need to form a partnership with others. When we strive to be open to suggestion and trust our fellow man, years of negative relations with others can melt away. We find this applicable in all aspects of our lives, including job, family and friends.

We bring this presentation of the Twelve Steps to a close here. This program is not a theory, we have to live it if we want recovery in our lives. Progress is what we strive for and in time our obsessive-compulsiveness will be relieved if we keep coming back to give this way of life a chance to work for us.

We Can Do Together...

I have been a member of OCA for almost a year, and I am also a member of another twelve-step group. In my other group, we do a lot of socializing – we go out on weekends for beach parties, picnics, etc. I thought, "Wouldn't it be nice to do that with my OCA group, too?" Then I started thinking about all of the reasons why I thought it could never work out for us. Just imagine it - the "checkers" would never get there on time ... lots of us afraid to drive (we might hit cars or people and then we might not know for sure if we'd done it ...) ... some of us don't like to collect money (afraid we might steal it accidentally, or become contaminated from handling it) ... and the people with contamination fears might worry about eating food prepared by the rest of us... "it would be a disaster!" I thought. At that point I began to feel even more isolated and sorry for myself...

Then I remembered my experience as a "shabbas goy." When I worked in campus ministry years ago, I became friends with the campus rabbi. We shared our traditions, and one day he asked me to be his "shabbas goy." Literally, this means "sabbath gentile," and it's a non-Jew who can help out a Jew in special circumstances when the Jew is unable to do something because of Jewish law. For example, a shabbas goy might turn on the lights or write something down for a Jewish friend on the sabbath day when orthodox Jews aren't permitted to do anything that constitutes "work." Or, my rabbi friend asked me to help him for one holy week when he was supposed to surrender all his possessions. He sold me everything he owned for a dollar for the week. I was flattered that he would share his traditions with me, and honored that he would trust me with all his worldly possessions (and knew that I would willingly sell them all back to him the next week for the same price!).

We at OCA do the same thing. Unlike orthodox Jews, who choose, as a community, to follow one set of laws, we in OCA each seem to suffer under a set of rigid and often tyrannical personal "laws" which bind us. Our personal laws are often shared by few others we know, if any. But we do have different laws, and in OCA we share a common understanding that enables us to transcend our differences (and sometimes even the laws themselves!) So maybe we can't all get to the beach or a picnic on time, or handle money, or feel comfortable driving or cooking, but each one of us can do something; and we can actually admit to each other what we cannot do. So we COULD have a picnic, and actually be honest with each other. Imagine a social event where we would not have to lie (about why we were late, or why we don't want to participate in something), or avoid things, or disappear at certain uncomfortable times for us – a social event we don't avoid altogether because of our OCD! A social event where we could be ourselves? What a picnic that would be! I think we can do it. Together.

(1)
Once Was Never Enough

I've heard in the meetings that some people "acquire" Obsessive Compulsive Disorder (OCD). It seems that I was just born with it. I remember that during my childhood I arranged my toys in a particular pattern – not to be disturbed by anyone.

Perfectionism, an impossible goal, became my goal. In school, I managed to excel since I always completed my assignments before their due dates. My studies assumed an important part of my life which is why I finished college with the highest of honors and graduated professional school to enter into my chosen field.

During those years, the main manifestations of my OCD were checking, counting and fear of dirt and contamination. Somehow I managed to keep it "under control" because I was so busy with my studies. I figured that this "quirk" in my personality enabled me to excel in school since I was able to "plan my life" better than most people.

I little realized how my OCD would turn on me. During those college years, I developed the acne problem common to adolescence. This normal condition turned into something very abnormal for me. I would spend countless hours picking at my skin until it bled. Mirrors assumed an important role in my life – almost every spare moment found me in front of one.

All personal efforts to stop failed. Removing the mirrors from the walls or disconnecting the lights became easily reversible. I found myself picking late into the evening despite the protests of my family. This ritual became my master, no human could stop me.

This intensified for about five years during which I sought professional help. Therapy produced no results for me. Hypnosis, biofeedback and a nutritionist were ineffective. Although my OCD was assuming a more important role in my life, I somehow managed to keep my job and my family. Those closest to me stuck by me no matter how hopeless the problem appeared to be while I on the other hand, became very angry and sarcastic. I would often argue with people needlessly, defending my right to continue this behavior since my OCD seemed to be bothering them more than it was bothering me - so I claimed. My denial was firmly embedded. I didn't want anyone to interfere with my OCD rituals. I didn't realize that I had an illness that I could not recover from alone, that I need-ed an outside source of strength.

My turning point came when someone who knew me well mentioned that my problem reminded him very much of an addiction, particularly alcoholism. At first I resisted this concept but gradually, after reading some of Alcoholics Anonymous' literature, I became convinced of the similarity. Both OCD and alcoholism are addictive, out-of-control, mis-guided searches for feelings of relief which only result in pain.

By attending A.A. meetings, I began to get some relief. However, I didn't do what the program suggested, including practicing the 12 Steps, sponsorship, phone calls. I guess I wasn't really ready to commit myself to something that might actually work. I still thought that I could handle this problem on my own.

Around the Fall of 1987 news of Obsessive Compulsive Disorder became a media event. People just like me were on T.V. and in the newspapers. OCD was becoming a household word. I really thought that by now a group of us would have gotten together to try to help each other. I was hoping for the creation of a group that based its recovery on the same 12

Steps that numerous other anonymous programs successfully use. Sadly, this was not the case. How could this be? Obviously, since this approach was helping me, it had to help others.

January 1988 saw the beginning of Obsessive Compulsive Anonymous (OCA). I thought I would be the last person interested in starting a group like this. I was too "busy" with my work and family. Besides, I needed the extra time to perpetuate my OCD.

Reluctantly, I saw my course. Either I work the program to the best of my ability or fall back into my old patterns. Obsessive Compulsive Anonymous allowed me to participate fully in the 12 Step way of life. I came to believe that my recovery was dependent on a Higher Power and that I could do His work by working with others with OCD who want the program.

OCA has brightened my life beyond my expectations. I am no longer a daily victim of my OCD. My episodes are far apart and less intense. I no longer feel like I'm on the edge in constant turmoil. I actually can enjoy peace of mind. The people whom I thought I had to change no longer need changing; they are who they are. I don't feel trapped by people, places or things. I have options today. I participate in life – I'm no longer a victim of it. I look forward to my meetings today because I have a chance to share with those who uniquely understand and will not criticize or judge me. I am also privileged to watch the newcomers who see that this is available to them, too, if they are willing to give the program half the time and energy that they gave their OCD. As long as the Higher Power requires my participation in OCA I will gratefully pass on the gift which has been given to me.

Postscript

Since first writing this story, things in my life have changed even more. Recovery from OCD has proven challenging since experiencing life has proven more real than hiding in my rituals.

My relations with other people (especially my spouse) were strained in early recovery. I guess that when two people have spent years of their lives trying to control the OCD, they then find themselves left with just each other once the disease is no longer the central theme of their existence together. Therefore, adjustments must be made. I've spoken with many people in OCA who have gone through such "adjustments" and I'm glad that I'm not alone.

Recently, I've also had to face the biological realities associated with OCD. My four-year-old daughter had an "acute" OCD episode. I can only describe this experience as terrifying. Seeing the manifestations of this illness in someone so young and so close to me has been extremely painful. I know, though, that this program and knowledgeable professionals are there for her with insight and help that wasn't available to me when I was her age.

As a result, her recovery is nothing short of remarkable. She has recently been able to face her worst fears and walk through them. Most importantly, my wife and I have reset our priorities as parents. We have come to realize that a child's freedom to make mistakes is more important than getting a stain on a new dress or skinning a knee from running too fast. The *last* thing that a child with OC tendencies needs is to feel that she or he has to be "perfect."

As a parent recovering from OCD, my innate tendency to overprotect her has been replaced with looser guidelines and letting go of my control. Since I see the world as a safer place, now she can also interpret *her* world that way. Her mistakes are now treated as experiences to learn from instead of only things necessary to correct.

Introducing the concept of a loving God to our child has allowed her to experience the unconditional love we feel for her regardless of her shortcomings. We've allowed her to recognize that God loves us all, even when we mess up.

I feel that it is also important to mention the changes that I've experienced in my relationships with other people as my recovery continues. By working diligently, my wife and I have been able to renew our closeness which was torn by the OCD. Things are better between us now than they have ever been. My parents and I have been able to forgive each other and the special feelings that I had for them as a child are returning.

I am fortunate that working the Twelve-Step program of OCA has dramatically reduced my OCD. Because it is such a vicious disease, I was willing to do *anything* (including starting OCA) to get relief from it.

To further my recovery, I've recently begun taking medication commonly used for OCD. I feel that *my* recovery in the Twelve-Step program can be enhanced by availing myself of all the possible avenues of relief from OCD.

I am grateful for what OCA has done for me and with God's help, others can find the relief that I've been privileged to enjoy.

(2)
Sobriety From OCD

I think I've been putting off writing my story for so long because I just don't want to remember the pain I went through with the OCD. I'm experiencing such good recovery that I almost don't want to remember the pain, but I know that by writing this story and having it appear in this book I might help others to recover and maybe someone out there can identify with what I've gone through.

I had a rough childhood. My father was a very abusive alcoholic, emotionally and sometimes physically. I was always a nervous, frightened child who felt different from everyone else. I also felt that there was something wrong with me. I probably suffered from OCD as far back as I can remember. I became obsessed with different things, but I was mostly obsessed with my appearance and my bodily functions, odors and other things like that. I can also remember having an obsession with the curse word "shit" which got really bad as time went on. When I was a child my mother literally washed my mouth out with soap for saying that word. I can't say for sure if that was definitely related to my obsession, but as I think back I realize that it probably was; it doesn't take a psychiatrist to figure that one out.

That obsession probably lasted for a good year and it was torture. I was always afraid that I was going to blurt it out or that someone knew that I was thinking that word and I would get banished to hell or something like that, for having that word in my mind. It produced a lot of panic attacks, isolation and fear. Somehow, I barely made it through high school. I graduated, got married and got a job, but was always nervous and fearful.

My main obsession, though, was with my facial expression. I focused mostly on my eyes and was extremely self-conscious. I believed that they looked bizarre and that one eye was larger than the other. I checked them in the mirror hundreds of times a day to see if they actually looked as bizarre as I thought they did. Of course, I believed that they looked a certain way and was convinced of that. Then, as the years passed, the job I worked at for about ten years was coming to an end because the company was merging with a larger company. Since I don't take well to change, I became very frightened. I think that people with OCD are almost allergic to change, whether it's positive or negative change.

Until that point my OCD consisted primarily of obsessional thoughts. I started to compulsively stare at the ground or roll my eyes in my head, cross my eyes or even make distorted faces at people. It went hand in hand with the eyes and the facial expressions. I actually had conversations with people (which I desperately tried to avoid) in which I could barely concentrate on what they were saying to me. Instead, during the conversation, I was thinking about what my face looked like. This caused me a lot of anxiety, fear, and self-hatred as well as embarrassment. This just seemed too idiotic to me, and yet I couldn't stop. The more I tried to control it and relax my face, the worse it became. I bought every self-help book imaginable, I tried psychotherapy and I was in a hospital for a month. At the age of 16 I was prescribed medication for severe migraine headaches. I believe that these headaches were actually the result of the stress in my home caused by my father's alcoholism and the anxiety that I felt from OCD. I also tried bio-feedback and hypnosis. I tried everything from diets to exercise programs to combat this OCD. Some things helped me temporarily but it always seemed that the OCD would come back even stronger and worse than it was before. Whenever the OCD seemed to be somewhat in remission, it would inevitably come back even harder.

Somehow I gave birth to two daughters, 18 months apart. After the birth of my second child I began developing an obsession with the untrue notion that I was yelling out obscenities and didn't hear myself.

I was so withdrawn and into my own little world that the only time I left my home was when I had to go food shopping or take care of other necessities. I even wore sunglasses so that no one would see my eyes. I was a mess. The OCD had gotten so bad that I was afraid that if I left my home and I was out yelling obscenities, which I never was, I would be locked up and my kids would be taken away. I had all of these horrible fears. When I shopped, I clung to the shopping cart for dear life with my sweaty palms, ready to break the cart in half. I just wanted to get this trauma over with and go home in the security of my house.

The OCD seemed to hit me harder when I was outside of my home. In my house I had a feeling of safety, but when I was around other people it was really difficult to function.

I also had other obsessive behaviors with housecleaning. I was always either up on a ladder scrubbing down walls, or mopping the floors. I also became very obsessed with my children. When they played I didn't like having toys about and I liked everything tidied up. I was just like a patrol person around my home. No one could relax or live comfortably in this home. I just patrolled around all the time picking up lint from the floor or cleaning up toys that my kids wanted to play with. They weren't allowed to have them out because I got upset when things were out of order.

For a while the obsession with the eyes and the compulsion to make faces got very bad. I couldn't look at a person without doing something strange with my face or my eyes. Often, I was staring so intently at the floor that it looked as though I was going to collapse. I tortured myself afterward and felt such self-hatred. Thinking back, I believe that the OCD got so bad that I was losing sleep at night. I did what they caution a person against in A.A.. I didn't HALT and I got too *Hungry, Angry, Lonely* and *Tired.* I was always very tired because I was nursing my youngest daughter and my sleep was broken up by the feedings. I was walking around like a zombie with these fears and compulsions.

I finally hit rock bottom about three years ago. Everything had gotten so bad that I remember sitting in the corner of my bedroom thinking about killing myself. I was seriously contemplating suicide because I couldn't live the way I was living another day.

I felt that I was an awful mother because I just wasn't there for my kids. I started scolding my oldest daughter and found myself always angry at her. I knew it was my self-hatred projected onto this child and I felt that I was the worst mother in the world. I felt that I was insane and that there was something wrong with my brain. I believed that I would really be doing everyone a favor by just killing myself.

I was a very angry person with no belief in God or any Higher Power. I was hateful toward everybody and I had no friends. While reading the newspaper one afternoon a few days after that night I came across an announcement for the 12-step program of Recoveries Anonymous. They used the word "obsessions" and referred to suffering with these obsessions or any other self-destructive behavior. I called and spoke to a woman who later became my sponsor.

I began going to meetings once a week but I went in there like I went into so many other things that I had tried. I was very skeptical, especially when they talked about a Higher Power or

God. I thought spirituality meant religion. I was very, very leery but this woman said to me, "What do you have to lose? You've tried everything else. Just give it a fair shot and then decide." So, I thought to myself... "I'll try this. This is my last straw. If this doesn't work I will kill myself and then I will have known I tried everything."

So I started going to meetings, although in the beginning I refused to read the book *Alcoholics Anonymous*. I thought it was ridiculous and that my father should have read this book but not me. I did not have an alcohol problem. I thought that for a while until little by little I could hear that my personality was that of an alcoholic.

I just did not click onto alcohol as my obsession. I started reading the book and just kept going to meetings. The woman who I had spoken to over the telephone became my sponsor. I went to a workshop to learn more about the 12 steps and I started to think, "Well, you know, there is something to this." I wrote my resentment list and realized that everybody and anybody that I had ever known was on that list. I wondered if it could be all these people or if it could be me. Could all of these people be so bad? I realized that there were a lot of things that I did to others that made them treat me in certain ways. There were also a lot of things in my past that I really had to look at and examine.

My actions were not the best, so I started to make amends to people that I had harmed. I began to take an inventory every day. I also started praying every night to my Higher Power, who I defined as Nature. I feel that I really connect with Nature as a power greater than myself that I can tap into. I didn't try to analyze the Program.

When I asked a lot of questions, the people in the rooms told me, "Try not to overanalyze. Just try to work the steps to the best of your ability, and try to take it a day at a time." I started to meditate and I read a lot of other books that were suggested by another fellowship. I read the book entitled *Sermon on the Mount* which I really related to. It just seemed to make so much sense to me. I believe that after I finished reading that book I had a spiritual awakening of sorts and it was the turning point for me.

Also, after I had made some amends I began experiencing a peace of mind and serenity in my life that I had never known before. Anyone with OCD knows that feeling of the mind being on overdrive and not concentrating on anything. There is no peace in that state; it's constant. I was even dreaming the OCD.

I started to get periods of peace of mind. When I first joined the Program I said the serenity prayer over and over again. That seemed to help me a great deal. I remember writing it out and keeping it on a little card in my car and on my refrigerator. This really helped me. I started experiencing the OCD lifting and I began to have friends, which I had never had years ago. Back then I couldn't handle having anyone in my home. It was just too stressful and disruptive and caused me too much anxiety.

I met some really great people through the Program and I started to allow them into my home. I realized little by little that nothing terrible would happen. There is also a section with the promises in the "Big Book" that says that "fear of people will leave us." I had a big star next to that line because fear of people was a really big issue for me. This fear was starting to lift though and I was now able to have a conversation with a person without that self-consciousness and constant thinking about myself.

I started experiencing recovery and I knew that this was

the answer for me. I just knew it; there was definitely something to this that wasn't like all those other things I had tried. This program was the answer. It was freedom and sanity. This was what I knew in my heart would be the answer for me.

Through Recoveries Anonymous I met OCA's founder. He called me one night and said that he was starting another fellowship called OCA and that he knew a little bit about my symptoms and my disease. At that time though there wasn't much talk about OCD. It wasn't "labeled."

I started going to two meetings per week and I think that was another turning point for me. It seemed like doubling up on the meetings really sped up my recovery process. I recommend to people that join these programs to try to get to more than one meeting a week; to try to get to as many meetings as possible, especially in the beginning when they're really suffering.

Then OCA started to develop and we began to realize that there are so many people with OCD. Suddenly, all of this information about the disease started becoming publicized. It feels so wonderful that this book is now being written and that people can come out of the closet about their OCD since the nature of this illness is to want to hide it because you feel like such a freak and that you're insane.

Now I'm meeting such wonderful people – all types of people. Our groups consist of doctors, teachers and all sorts of people that one would think just wouldn't have problems like this. They're really normal in all other aspects except for the OCD. Like we always say in the meetings, "It's [the OCD] like a monkey on the back that is always there."

I've really come so far though. I've made all of these friends and I no longer am gripped by the obsession with my eyes. I feel that it's totally lifted. I do realize though that this is a program of recovery and I will never be cured. I must continue to practice these steps to the best of my ability for the rest of my life or the disease can come back at me. I really do believe that.

There's a lot of talk about OCD being caused by a chemical imbalance in the brain. My personal theory about this is that it is possibly a chemical imbalance, but I believe that we trip the chemicals off with our emotions and our reactions. I believe that people with OCD hold on to resentments much more than the "average, normal person." People with OCD are more sensitive than other people, but by practicing the twelve steps, a person can come to like this more peaceful way of life. It's a character change in one's reactions to the things that happen. In other words, we no longer overreact to things because we're more centered. I think through the Program we keep this middle, average type road and we no longer get into those situations where we're mulling over things and we're holding onto resentments. We can keep our peace of mind.

I just know that the Program works and I love it. I do find that at times it's very hard though to stick with it because it really goes against today's society. It's a very "me, me, me" type of society and I believe we must also work with others to keep our "sobriety." We have to think of others every day and how we can be helpful to them. Sometimes, that's not easy to do. We want to be selfish and we want to go about and do our own thing, but we have to keep others in our minds. I'm grateful that I'm a part of OCA so that I have the opportunity to help others recover from OCD.

(3)

OCA Offered More Than OCD Relief

Obsessive Compulsive Disorder (OCD) has many different symptoms. I'm 21 and I have OCD. I experience the same pain as anyone else who has this disorder. Each person can have different symptoms, but we all experience the same kind of pain.

OCD not only hurts a person spiritually, mentally, and physically, but it also affects an individual's personality. Now I realize that I have many character defects. My OCD altered my perceptions and I became a selfish, uncaring walking time bomb. I was a very irritable person who could flare up in a second. In short, my personality was warped.

For as long as I can remember I've had OCD. It started out slowly and was not really dominating my life. I did little things like counting and checking. Eventually, though, things got worse. At first I thought my rituals were just bad habits. I tried to control my compulsions which only made them worse. Since I was a perfectionist I thought it was "normal" to check to make sure that everything in my closet was in order. At first I had spent only a few minutes checking, but eventually when things got really bad, I'd open and close the closet door about thirty times and then do the same with my bedroom door. I'd close it over and over again. I once opened and closed that door at least fifty times. When I finished that ritual, I knocked very hard on the door many times to make sure that it was closed. Then I would go downstairs only to have to go back up to make sure the door was closed. I used to cry a lot while I was performing my rituals. When I entered Obsessive Compulsive Anonymous (OCA) I felt hopeless.

I found out about the OCA program from a newspaper service column. Because the Program discusses the idea of a Higher Power, introduction into the group may be a bit difficult for some. This Higher Power doesn't necessarily have to be a conventional God or a religious figure. Your Higher Power can be the OCA group, or even nature. The main point is that it's a power outside of yourself. Many people may get turned off by that concept, but it's really important to stay as open-minded as possible and have the willingness to take actions toward recovery from OCD.

I didn't have a problem actually choosing a Higher Power of my understanding, but I still couldn't believe that an abstract power could relieve me of my obsessions if I couldn't do it myself. I was wrong!!

The Program also suggested that I read the literature, make phone calls and go to meetings. Basically, that I work and live in the 12 steps of recovery. However, initially I only worked some of these steps in my life. I didn't like the idea of making telephone calls, but sick people usually don't like healthy suggestions. I went to meetings and I sometimes read the books.

It took a while before I got any results at all from working the Program, and this made me feel worse. However, after two months I started feeling the effects of going to the meetings and OCD recovery. I finally had relief and felt so free and so good.

Not everyone is that fortunate. Don't be discouraged if your OCD symptoms don't subside immediately and you don't begin to see the results of recovery quickly. It takes longer for some people than for others. I know people who have taken two months to a year to "get the Program." It's worth the wait though. I know I'm not finished with my recovery even though I've been in the Program for over a year. I try to work on my recovery every day.

When I have my "bad days" now, it's usually because I'm not working some aspect of my Program. As someone once told me, OCA is not a cure, but it sure offers, and gives, help and relief from OCD. If a person practices the principles of this simple, but not easy, program, that person can be sure to get results, even it it takes a while.

I know that I have gotten relief because now I do make the phone calls, read my books, listen, and often follow suggestions from other OCA members, as well as take my own inventory.

If you are wondering what it means to "take an inventory," to me it means getting rid of the time bomb inside of me as well as acknowledging, admitting and ultimately getting rid of my harmful resentments. The Big Book of Alcoholics Anonymous even states that resentments are the number one offender and a person must part with them if that person is to live a life of recovery. After one year I'm finally starting to let go of my resentments even though I never *really* wanted to get rid of them. Parting with my resentments towards other people has not only created a greater peace within myself, but has also enabled me to become a more caring person.

The program recommends that I listen to people and take suggestions. When someone suggested that I lead a meeting, I felt that I would actually faint if I spoke in front of a group. I took this person's suggestion and did it anyway. Now I'm very glad that I did. It's uncomfortable for me to lead a meeting because I have a hard time talking in front of crowds. However, if I want to recover, I must do what I don't always want to do, such as leading meetings and making telephone calls. I've also learned that these calls not only help me, but they help the other person too.

It's amazing what the Program has done for me. This is a simple Program but it's definitely not an easy one. If I can help another OCD sufferer to feel better simply by making a phone call or saying something at a meeting, I feel great and at peace. Before, I just wanted things for myself and didn't care about anyone else. It's in helping others that I can stay in recovery. I must give it away in order to keep it ... that feels good. I am so much better off than I was last year. I'm not saying that I'm perfect because I now know that I will never be perfect. I still have many things to work on. I get lazy and I have my "bad days" too, but if I didn't have the Program I might be in an insane asylum now. The Program works if you work it. All a person needs is an open mind, willingness and the desire to recover from OCD.

Even now I sometimes wait for results if a new obsession or compulsion appears. The best part though is that I have a terrific program that combats all aspects of my OCD. The Program is always there and it works. I can say this because I've experienced it. When I turn my OCD over to my Higher Power I get amazing results. When I work this Program, not only does my OCD become more manageable, but I live in a more positive way.

Even after I entered OCA I became afraid of contracting AIDS. However, I was relieved of this obsession after only three days of becoming involved in the Program. I don't think I will ever be cured of OCD, but I do believe that we can all live in recovery from this disorder and become better, happier and sane people.

I feel blessed to have OCD since it's because of this painful disorder that I have found the OCA Program and have become a better, less selfish and more caring person. So, the bottom line is that a person can live a life of recovery from OCD if that person gives himself to this simple Program.

(4)
It Took 12 Steps to Live with "13"

I was born on November 14,1963. I have had OCD for about seven years and I have suffered tremendously.

I was approximately twenty years old when I began to develop a fear of the number thirteen. Whenever I saw the number thirteen, in any form, I felt totally contaminated. This included the time appearing on a clock, such as 3:13, as well as 1:00 P.M. which I converted in my mind into the thirteenth hour. I felt totally contaminated when the change I received was 13 cents or 13 dollars, as well as when it was the 13th day of the month or when I read words consisting of 13 letters. The pain brought on by this feeling of contamination consumed my entire being.

For the first five years I felt that I could conquer this fear on my own. I was never more wrong. I tried to convince myself that I could handle this... that it would go away... it didn't. Instead, it began to develop into some sort of monster that now controlled more and more of me. One day, while at the barber for a haircut, I had 13 dollars in my possession. At that time I thought nothing of this. Immediately after having my hair cut I felt that I was totally consumed with evil contamination. The only means that I felt I could use to rid myself of this evil feeling was to continue to get my hair cut. I was now going to the barber every 14 days or less. Not only did I begin to look ridiculous, but my barber could not understand why I felt that I needed to get my hair cut so often. A peach had more fuzz on it. I felt embarrassed, ashamed and completely lost. I knew I could no longer attempt to handle this problem on my own. Was I crazy? I wondered what was wrong with me. Do other people ever get like this? Who could I talk to? Who would believe me? I began to think that I must be crazy or perhaps I had a brain tumor. I knew that I had to seek help .. but where would I start? I turned to my local telephone directory to see if anything was listed beginning with the word "phobia." Yes, there was a name for my condition. It's known as Obsessive Compulsive Disorder (OCD).

I was lucky. I found a therapist who referred me to a psychiatrist and I began treatments with both of these professionals.

Initially, I was seeing my therapist once a week and my psychiatrist every other week. At least four times a week I was attending a support group for people that suffer from OCD. They too offered me tremendous support. After 16 months of seeing my therapist, I was able to discontinue these visits. Presently, I see my psychiatrist once a month. I attend group a minimum of 2 times per week.

Sharing my feelings with other OCD sufferers has helped me realize that I am not alone. Approximately 4 million Americans suffer from some sort of Obsessive Compulsive Disorder. I was fortunate to realize, when I did, that I needed help. I'm eternally grateful to all the people who have worked, and continue to work, with me to help me conquer this illness. I am especially grateful to my parents for standing by me with their continued love and support. I am also extremely grateful to the people at my Thursday evening Obsessive Compulsive Anonymous (OCA) meeting. This group of people whom I love very much has helped me tremendously ... they've saved my life.

Through the miracles of modern medicine, therapy, and OCA, I am now able to feel relief from my obsession. My life has turned around completely, but that does not mean that at this time I am cured because I am not. I will always go to OCA meetings because there I have a fellowship that I can count on.

(5)
One 'Strand' At A Time

I can't think of any one time or single place that it all began. I only know that my rebirth happened last March, 1989. I can remember as a child performing the ritualistic behavior of bumping my head all night on my pillow. My mother used to come into my room during the middle of the night to wake me up to stop me from bumping my head which shook the bed frame and woke up my parents. Since I was asleep, I didn't even know that I was doing it. I felt that I just had to bump my head on the pillow. Consequently, I developed a crooked nose which was reshaped when I had a rhinoplasty at the age of 16.

I can remember twisting my hair from 7 years old until I was about 11 or 12 when I recall pulling it out by the roots and watching it fall on the floor strand by strand, pile by pile, not really wondering anything about it. I just knew that I had to do it and it felt good. It wasn't until I was around 14 or 15 years old that I started getting bald spots. My mother noticed them and began getting concerned. Since I told her that I would stop, I became very secretive and pulled my hair when no one was around.

I can't remember too much about the whens, the hows and the whats during my teenage years, but I do remember that I had the worst self-image in the entire world and I hated myself. When I was 15, I enrolled in a private school to improve my grades. I was a very ugly teenager and the boys in school always laughed at me.

It's hard to think of all of the different times and places of pain and humiliation, wearing wigs and trying to say, "I do this thing." I remember going to the hairdressers who often said, "I don't recall ever seeing anything like this before." Sometimes I wished I had cancer just so I'd have an excuse. Although there were a couple of understanding hairdressers who would work with me, there were others that were mean and would just insult me.

I guess the worst period was from about 15 to 25 years old. I just kept pulling and pulling and it got worse and worse. When I was in college, the spots on either side of my head above my ears were awful. I never wanted to pull the hair in the back of my head, but I always pulled on the sides, and sometimes on the top of the crown and in the front. I thought it was just a habit, like sucking your thumb, nail biting or smoking cigarettes, except I just couldn't stop. I suppose the worst part was that I couldn't find anyone else who also did this.

Consequently, I felt worthless because I believed that no man would want to date a woman with a bald head. I was very emotionally immature and sheltered throughout my whole life. I never wanted to do anything or go anywhere, nor did I excel in anything. My parents really didn't encourage me to do anything so I just sort of grew up feeling very mixed up inside. I remember that each time I reached out to somebody for help, love or understanding, the door would slam shut in my face. Naturally, that didn't help to alleviate my compulsion.

I had a couple of close friends but I wasn't popular and I certainly wasn't pretty. I'll never forget the day in sixth grade when my mother sent me out of the house with a plaid skirt and a striped blouse. When I got to school the kids laughed at me all day because my clothes were so uncoordinated.

I guess I was always jealous of my mother because she was so beautiful and I wasn't. I suppose you could say that trichotillomania [hair pulling] was partly self-mutilation because I knew that I would never be pretty so I felt that I

64

might as well continue to pull my hair out. No matter how many theories there may be about this, all I know is that I couldn't stop pulling my hair out. My mother yelled and screamed at me and I cried because I couldn't stop pulling my hair. She sent me to a psychiatrist who told me what it was, but didn't offer any good suggestions, behavior therapy or other treatments to help me stop pulling my hair. I guess I can't really blame him though because at that time, twenty years ago, they didn't know anything about this stuff. Sometimes I think back and wonder if Howard Hughes would have lived a more fulfilling life had medical research been more advanced. Would any of us have lived a more fulfilling life? But I can't look back; I just have to take my experience and move on.

I want to reach out to other people, to the little girl who's pulling her hair out and say, "there's hope. You're not alone." One of our OCA groups in Pittsburgh is strictly for people with trichotillomania. Through this group, I've developed a network of other hair pullers and their families. It's been one of the most rewarding things I've ever done. I've made friends with a 16 year old member and another person who's 11, who are very severely stricken with this disease. I keep telling them not to give up because as research progresses there will hopefully be a solution to this problem. I've told them that I'm going to just keep praying for them until something happens in God's time because I know what they're going through. The change happened for me and I somehow believe that it's going to happen for them.

I think a lot about my OC family of checkers, washers, car drivers who are afraid that they've run somebody over, ruminators, contamination obsessors, perfectionists, people who want to be in control, people who constantly take their clothes on and off, people who are constantly picking their feet or their fingers and those people who are still in pain who I haven't met yet because they're too sick to come to group. I think about my OC family constantly. One might say that I obsess about OCD, but when a person doesn't know what he or she has, and after 35 years finally finds out that there are millions of people out there who have OCD and do the same things, it's like suddenly finding out that you have polio and then learning that Dr. Salk developed a vaccine for it.

When I think of all the research that's going on now, I realize that the children who've got OCD and the adults that suffer from symptoms don't have to suffer through years of agony with this disease any more. Nevertheless, the OCD life is a lonely life until one meets the OC family. I can honestly say that the past 12 months have been both the greatest and worst months of my life. They have been the greatest because of all the wonderful people that I've met and the work that I've been able to do to get the word out to other people with OCD. I marvel at all of the different sufferers who I've been able to find, those who have found us, and some of the recoveries that are starting to happen. There is nothing in the world more fantastic and helpful to a person's recovery than watching another sufferer recover.

I guess the painful part is when a person begins going through his or her own changes and starts to recover it's hard for other people, whether it be friends, co-workers, acquaintances, family, and especially one's spouse or significant other because the person that they fell in love with is no longer the same person.

When a person is part of a 12 step program, that person becomes completely new once the recovery process begins. The Program just totally turns a person's life around, and it's very hard to continue a relationship because that person is just not the same as before. In that respect, these past 12 months have been the worst because I know recovery work is what I want to do for the rest of my life. At 36 finding myself suddenly turning around and saying to my husband, "I know what I'm going to do" is very scary, especially when he doesn't suffer with OCD and doesn't understand what I'm going through.

I've been in remission since August 4th, 1989. My basic avenues of recovery have been my faith in my Higher Power, which for me is God, my OC family, my support groups and lastly, my medication.

Through my recovery I've learned not to try to be such a perfectionist but just to be me. I know that I will never give up my faith or my OC family; they've meant my rebirth. I especially appreciate the work and support that we've all gotten from the OC Foundation, Obsessive Compulsive Anonymous and the Pittsburgh Self-Help Group Network. The tireless members of these organizations have shown me the way to finding new energies and a new person in myself, who's always learning, growing and open to new ideas.

(6)
It Works

I have suffered from OCD since early childhood. I remember at an early age having to memorize TV commercials and going over them in my mind before going to sleep at night. I also had stuffed animals that I had to arrange in a particular order each day. In my way of thinking I did these things to keep something bad from happening to my parents. At about the age of fourteen I had a fear that my parents would turn into animals if I did not think positive thoughts about them. I have since learned that this is called magical thinking.

In the afternoons, after school, I went to my room, closed my door and went through thoughts and feelings that I felt needed to be straightened out in my mind. Perfectionism was involved with the OCD too. I was trying to actually make myself have good thoughts and feelings.

I married immediately after high school at an early age. My husband was a sick person also. He abused me throughout the marriage. This relationship lasted for eleven years until I finally left with our two beautiful children. My self-esteem was already low from the OCD, but now it was even lower from the abuse. I started using alcohol to help alleviate fears and worries.

I met my present husband about a year later. He had an alcohol problem too. We've been married for ten years and he has recently stopped drinking. My drinking is also under control. I used alcohol as a self-medication for the OCD. Although I got a little relief with the alcohol sometimes, at other times the liquor just made the OCD worse. As a person with OCD, the depression that alcohol caused was devastating to me since depression is usually associated with the disease also.

I started seeing a psychiatrist over a year ago who advised me to attend A.A. (Alcoholics Anonymous) meetings to help the OCD and the alcohol problem. I went to a lot of meetings, enjoyed the fellowship and learned a bit about the twelve-steps.

A friend who has OCD and I started an OCA group several months ago in our area. About seven people attend the meeting regularly. The fellowship is great and together we are learning to use the steps in our lives. As we grow, learn, and attend these meetings, they are becoming a great benefit to all of us in the group. Recently my OCD symptoms went into remission. I owe my thanks to the OCA program through which I was able to make the changes necessary to further my recovery.

(7)
Stop Worrying So Much

I know that I have never in my life really felt peace. I also know that at every moment there's been at least one thing that I worried about intensely or something that I got "stuck on." For months I worried and worried about this one thing. It was usually something that I felt guilty about doing when I was a small child. Perhaps I threw a piece of litter down the sewer, picked up a dirty clothespin off the bargain store floor and carried it home, or got a postcard for the discount price when the others were not on sale. These things produced years of worry with the fear that the police would come after me. The ultimate fear though, sitting in the back of my mind, was that I would someday end up being executed for murder. This fear was so frightening to me that I didn't want to go on vacations to states that had the death penalty just in case something happened. I knew at a very young age just which states these were.

I don't think I had a lot of rituals as a child. It was mostly the thoughts that drove me crazy. I do remember, though, holding my breath or spitting when I passed a cemetery. Also, every night when I was young, as early as I can remember, I went over a litany with my mom in which I had to ask her, "Is there nothing to worry about? Even a, b, c (whatever the specifics were at the time?)" She'd say, "Yes, there's nothing to worry about."

For as long as I can remember I have been afraid of being alone with my thoughts. Family vacations were awful because of the long period of time in the car when I couldn't read (being carsick or it was dark), nobody was talking and I was left alone for long periods of time with just my own thoughts. It was awful.

At home, when I went to sleep I used to listen to records from all the great musicals. Then I memorized all of them, even the really complicated ones like the opening to *The Music Man* with all of its parts ... I still remember a lot of it. I also remember when we went to see the total eclipse on Cadillac Mountain and they talked so much about not looking directly at the sun during the eclipse that I then started worrying that maybe I had done it wrong. All night in the tent I kept getting terrified and asking them to turn on the lights. Each time I was relieved to find that I wasn't blind (yet). But a few minutes later it would seem to get darker and darker... my brother got pretty annoyed with me.

Anyway ... does this mean that I have OCD??? Is that what was going on all along? Maybe so. I guess it probably was. I have always just thought that I was a person who worried a lot. From my earliest teacher conferences (around kindergarten or first grade) all my teachers told my mom that I was doing great but that I had to stop worrying so much. (Apparently, I had announced to my kindergarten or first grade classmates during show-and-tell that an atom bomb had been discovered and we were all going to die.)

When I sought professional help later, in high school and college, the school psychologist and the chaplain told me that I just needed to stop worrying so much. I was so smart and so functional. I was the head of every school and I went to a top university. How disturbed could I really be?? I never knew HOW to stop worrying. I think I started to wonder, if I was O.K., then why was I so unhappy?

I have always looked at each of my worries as individual problems, but to say that I have OCD seems to say that maybe what seems to be the problem isn't as much the problem as the way my mind works and interprets things. That's confusing to me.

To say that I have a disease of sorts is really comforting in a way, if I could be cured. But I don't know what that would look like and I can't really imagine it. I am so used to feeling badly about myself that it actually feels somewhat sinful to TRY to feel better.

The idea in Obsessive Compulsive Anonymous that nobody, or nothing in particular is to blame for this is also a radically different idea for me. I've spent twelve years in therapy trying to understand myself. I've gotten support through the pain and I've learned to be more assertive and more articulate about my feelings. I don't regret any of the time I spent with good therapists, but nobody ever made the pain go away. I have never been able to stand on my own and take the pain, or make decisions for myself without actually going nuts. This has been a source of great shame. I had really hoped for the "Freudian Miracle"; that I would one day figure out what horrible thing happened in my early childhood that made everything go awry. I have always held a dream of hypnosis or regression therapy as a last resort...to just grit my teeth and go back there and find out what the hell it was and get *it* over with, no matter how painful it is. But what if there never was an *IT*?

Today I had a good morning and enjoyed spending time with my baby. The time flew and I didn't sit around in a slump wondering how I was going to get through the day. I started thinking that maybe I don't really have OCD. I haven't been obsessive in a while (since yesterday). But then I went out with the baby and while I was parking someone squeezed by. I heard a noise and I couldn't stop wondering if our cars had scraped, and would I know it if they had? If they had, was it my responsibility? Should I do anything about it?... and so on and so on. After I took the baby for her checkup, I called my husband from a pay phone (across the street where no one could hear what I was saying because they might either think I was a dangerous driver or else I was nuts for asking him) and just double checked with him. If I had talked to myself a lot, or had been in a better mood, I probably could have lasted without asking him and getting his reassurance. If not, perhaps I could have at least waited until he got home. It did give me peace right then and there to get it off my mind. I guess I must have OCD ...

I was asked to share my "experience, strength and hope" with readers of this book. I feel like I am a real beginner here. I don't know how my story will turn out, but I do have a great deal of hope, and I *CAN* talk about *that*. For the first time in my life I have found people who seem to understand the particular pain I have always carried with me. They know what I mean when I tell my story. While our particular obsessions may differ greatly, the pain, frustrations, fears and shame involved in having OCD seem to be strikingly similar for all of us. For the first time, I can admit to myself and to others the "crazy" thoughts and actions that take hold of my life. I can begin to feel what it is like not to feel shame. I can even enjoy being laughed at, lovingly, by people in the group who can point out the ridiculousness of my fears while they understand the depth of my pain and the grip that these fears have on my life. Between my psychiatrist, my therapist, the OCA group and ACOA (Adult Children of Alcoholics) group that I attend, I actually feel, for the first time, that I have a real support network. Each one of them supports my work with the others because they all have a similar philosophy. Each support system encourages me to do everything I can to work on my recovery by using behavior therapy, medication, the twelve steps and the support of the community. For the first time, I am beginning to hope there is something I can do to become freer, with the help of others, instead of just waiting for one obsession to replace another so I can have that temporary period of relief when I get rid of the old one. For the first time, I am beginning to hope for some sort of real healing. I am encouraged to transform my way of living and thinking, rather than weathering out each period of clinical depression and hoping that the next one will not come soon. For the first time, I am beginning to feel that I am not alone, and maybe I never need to be alone again.

(8)
From Fear to Faith

"You are not an alcoholic," the clinical psychologist stated firmly. "Yes, I am," I retorted. "Your problem is not alcohol." "Please don't tell me I'm not an alcoholic," I begged, then added, "It's taken me too long to get sober as it is." "You can believe you're an alcoholic if you want to, but I'm telling you alcohol is not your main problem."

That was December, 1976. I had been sober through the program of Alcoholics Anonymous for a year by then. I was living in a half-way house for alcoholic women and going to A.A. meetings daily. I was quite sore by the time I left the psychologist's office that afternoon. In fact, I had made up my mind that if she couldn't believe I was an alcoholic, I would not go back to see her.

My vocational rehabilitation counselor had difficulty understanding why I was so upset with the psychologist, and insisted I see her again. He assured me the doctor was sorry she'd upset me and would apologize to me; but I had to go back to see her again. She was treating me for my severe hand-washing compulsion and my fears of contamination. The odd thing about my visit with her that day was that she did not tell me what my main problem was – that I have Obsessive Compulsive Disorder.

I know today that the doctor was right – but only partially right. I am an alcoholic. I was unable to stop drinking when I wanted to. It took me almost two years in A.A. to be able to stop completely. But OCD is my main problem.

Looking back over my life, I have to admit that I have always been insecure and afraid. My earliest memory is one of fear. I was anxious and unable to relax, even as a child.

I was born in Pittsburgh, Pennsylvania, the third of seven girls. The family moved to Florida when I was five years old. My father is an alcoholic who got very violent when he drank, and my mother has had nervous problems. As a child I remember hearing stories about my mother being on the verge of a nervous breakdown when I was born. I heard gruesome accounts of the horrible pain I put my mother through, and how I resisted the doctors' best efforts to bring me into the world. I ended up feeling guilty just for being alive. Still I didn't blame my mother. Growing up, I thought she was a saint. She seemed so perfect. I wanted to be just like her. I was afraid of my father, as he made what I considered unreasonable demands on me and my sisters, expecting us to act like adults instead of children. We were often berated and whipped with belts. My parents fought constantly and I stayed upset over it. I was brought up Catholic and was a very religious child. I was well-liked by both my classmates and teachers at parochial school, despite my timidity.

My OCD surfaced around the age of eight. I was very obsessed with doing the right thing – always. I had a terrible fear of sinning, and constantly worried about displeasing God and going to hell. It seemed as though the harder I tried to be good, the worse I felt about myself. As the years went by, it seemed things just got worse. I found myself plagued with constant doubt. Going to confession on Saturday afternoon was a particular problem because no matter how thorough I had been, I never felt right (nor forgiven, for that matter) once I stepped out of the confessional. I was terrified that once I stepped outside the front door of the church I was going to drop dead on the steps. At first, I could resist going back into the church after confession, but as time went on I found myself going back and forth through the doorway without knowing why.

It was around this time that my hair pulling began. It started one day while I was sitting at my desk in school. I pulled out my hair at the crown, and then bit the roots off of each piece. Once I started, I was unable to stop when I wanted to. I ended up with bald spots on the top of my head, which I had to cover up. Later, I pulled out my eyebrows. I was so ashamed of myself, and could not understand why I couldn't stop pulling my hair.

At age twelve I decided I wanted to be a nun. My sixth grade teacher was such a wonderful one. I remember thinking that being a nun was probably the closest thing you could get to being a saint. I began saving my pennies in a coffee can so I could join the convent, because I knew my parents couldn't afford to send me.

Somewhere around this time, my parents divorced. At first, I really expected to feel better, as I no longer had to be around my father, and the threat of constant violence was gone. Instead, I began to fear that I was going insane. One night, out of desperation, I went to my mother and asked her to send me to see a psychiatrist. She said I didn't need one. There was little relief in her words. I was hurt and confused; I was sure she couldn't be blind to all my troubles. Didn't she know I was different? Couldn't she see the agony I was going through? Perhaps I'd been better at acting than I thought, as I had often tried to keep my problem a secret.

I began to drink when I turned seventeen years old. Up until then I'd been reluctant to drink (even at family dinners, etc.) because of the way alcoholism had destroyed my parents' marriage. But by seventeen my myriad fears and doubts were my constant companions. I couldn't shake them, and I stayed depressed much of the time. Drinking was fun at first, though I drank like an alcoholic from the start. It didn't take long for me to become really sick from alcohol; two months short of turning twenty-one, I attended my first A.A. meeting. Things did not go well for me in the beginning, and I drank again. I could see that the program worked for others, but I was not sure it could work for me.

During my early days in the program, I got professional help for the first time. I had counseling on and off, was put on medication, lived in a halfway house three different times, and attended meetings. Nothing seemed to help much. I ended up in the detox unit several times, the hospital twice for severe depression, and I overdosed once on a mixture of pills and booze. I also noticed I was spending an abnormal amount of time washing my hands and worrying about contamination.

I had my last drink on December 5, 1975. To this day, I believe that God was really looking out for me that night. I had set out to drink myself to death, for I thought I was fighting a losing battle. When I awoke the next morning, there were beer cans and half-burned cigarettes in the bed. I knew then that I had reached a turning point. I could not go on the way I was living. I needed help, and fast. I called A.A. again, and two dear ladies came out and talked to me, convincing me to go back into the halfway house and to get involved in A.A. I'm glad I listened to them, and am happy to say that I am now sober for a little over fourteen years.

I have only known about my Obsessive Compulsive Disorder for about a year now. I do not know why I was never told that I have OCD. Perhaps the psychiatrists just didn't know it. I found out what my problem was from watching the Phil Donahue show on OCD.

Throughout the process of recovery, my greatest fear was that I was going crazy. While Alcoholics Anonymous helped me to get my life together once I stopped drinking, it could not cure my OCD. After being sober about a year, my handwashing compulsion improved, but my OCD just expressed itself in other ways. I found myself constantly worrying about something bad happening, and then the checking began. I have been a checker for a very long time. There were times when my checking got so bad that I would be screaming inside, and at the same time I would beg God to take me or change me; I could not go on this way. In April, 1989, I made an appointment to see the doctor. I ended up telling him about my OCD. He seemed to have trouble understanding just how bad off I was. My husband had just been told he had a tumor and that it was most likely cancer. He was going to have to have surgery, and soon! I was a total wreck and was seeing danger in everything. The doctor gave me a prescription and I took it. At first it seemed to help, like the other medications I have had, only to make me feel worse the longer I took it. I stopped taking it.

I have always believed in God. My trouble since getting sober has been in trusting God to work things out for me. This has not stopped me from praying, and I cried with joy when we learned that my husband's tumor was benign.

My A.A. sponsor told me about the Recovery, Inc., Program, and encouraged me to attend. I went and felt the program was good. I did feel better when I went. Unaware of Obsessive Compulsive Anonymous' existence, I had wished there was a place for people like me to go for direct help with my specific illness.

Around this time, a letter appeared in the Ann Landers column in our local newspaper giving the address for the Obsessive Compulsive Foundation, as well as information on the work being done there. My husband brought the letter to my attention, encouraging me to write the Foundation. He insisted that they might be able to help me.

I put off writing for about a week. I'm not sure why, except perhaps I had some doubts that even they could help me. After all, everything else I had tried had failed. I still pulled my hair, breaking each strand into ten pieces, still feared contamination (though the handwashing was under control for the most part), still had terrible fears of death and/or of something horrible happening if I didn't recheck things, or if I drove an automobile.

My husband stood by me through it, though I'm sure it was hell for him at times. I never realized until recently how difficult it is for those who love us to live with us. It can't help but affect them, too.

The OC Foundation got me in touch with two wonderful women in the area also suffering from OCD. Up until then, I had never known but one other person with the disorder. Over the next few weeks, I kept in touch with these two OCD sufferers via the telephone. We all agreed we needed help, that it was a great feeling to know we weren't alone anymore, and that we needed the support of each other. Throughout this time, I talked on about how wonderful it would be if there was an organization like A.A. for OCD sufferers. None of us were aware then that OCA existed. The answer to my prayers came when a friend of mine in whom I had confided about my OCD brought me an article from *First Magazine*. There was a New York address for OCA in it. I was so excited that I wrote a letter to New York at once. Our kind friends in New York replied at once, and granted us permission to start a group in Florida.

Since I had helped start A.A. groups in Florida, I knew what needed to be done. I set about looking for a room we could meet in, and within two weeks, we had a place plenty large enough for the four of us to meet. I already had an A.A. Big Book, and the Twelve and Twelve, and my sponsor and friend volunteered to bring the coffee pot. On November 7, 1989, we met for the first time, in a church in Rockledge,

Florida. Thus, the Hope Group of Obsessive Compulsive Anonymous came into existence.

Today, I am truly grateful that OCA exists, and for the first time I have hope for a brighter future and a happy life. It is such a relief to know what is wrong with me, and that I can get better. I know how well the twelve steps work for alcoholism and I have faith that they will work just as well for my OCD. Although I am still very new to OCA, I have had a reduction in some of my symptoms, and my hair pulling compulsion has been lifted. I can relax, knowing everything is okay.

I am going to stay active in both my programs, as I believe that working with others will help me to get well. I know today that worry and trust do not go together. I have turned my life and will over to my Higher Power, and know that it is with Him that they rightly belong. After all, He didn't bring me this far to let go of me now.

(9)
My Secret

Outwardly, I appear to be a normal suburban housewife, your typical nice Italian Catholic girl married to a nice Jewish dentist. We have two healthy, terrific sons, a six-year-old and a four-year old. But inside, I carry a secret I've kept for over twenty-five years; I live the tortured life of a sufferer of OCD. Peace of mind, something most people take for granted, has not totally been mine since I was an adolescent (when this problem emerged).

My OCD has taken many forms, including obsessive thoughts, scrupulosity, excessive handwashing, excessive housecleaning, and excessive checking. This has made my life so unbearable that at times I've thought it would be better to be dead; then I might find the peace I so desperately want.

Like so many sufferers of OCD, I'm embarrassed and ashamed of the things I find it necessary to do. I've hidden as much of this behavior as I possibly could from friends, neighbors, co-workers and the people I love most. Like so many others with this affliction, I have been amazingly good at this deception. I've kept my OCD a secret from my sister-in-law, who is one of my closest confidantes and a psychiatric nurse, for approximately twenty-three years. I would tell someone I had to get something in my car, when my real purpose was to go check for the millionth time to see if the doors were locked. I would excuse myself to go to the bathroom, when my real purpose was to be alone so I could figure out whether an obsessive thought I had had was a mortal sin according to the teachings of the Roman Catholic Church.

Innately knowing this behavior is ludicrous hasn't stopped me. I'm compelled to do what I do. It hasn't even mattered that a compulsion is exhausting; I've still continued to do it. One night at the end of the school year, I stayed up practically all night, checking and rechecking my class attendance register to be sure it was correct. There were 180 boxes for each of my homeroom students, one box for each day of the school year. I had over twenty-five students. I had worked all day, then did this exhausting task and got to bed at approximately five-thirty in the morning. I got perhaps one and a half hours of sleep, got up and went to work the next day. To this day I don't think my husband has any idea I got so little sleep that night. I was six months pregnant with my first child at the time.

The hours I've spent agonizing over supposed sins I've committed are horribly painful for me to think about. I'll never forget the time I went to confession twice before I received communion on Easter Sunday. I've checked, rechecked then checked that I've rechecked store receipts. I've done this, not to be sure I wasn't overcharged or shortchanged, but rather, to be as positive as I possibly could be that I wasn't undercharged or given too much change.

OCD has prevented me from leading a full, productive and good life. I'm now in a Twelve-Step Program with others who share this vicious illness. Because of the people I've met in Obsessive Compulsive Anonymous, I'm not alone in my secret, painful world anymore. I've actually met and talked to people who the unbelievable has happened to: people who are in recovery from OCD.

The best possible life that I can dream of, hope for, and pray for is a life in recovery from OCD. I don't want more money, a bigger and better house, an expensive car; I just want freedom from this jail in my psyche. I want to be able to take my children to the playground, library, and soccer practice without constant worry. I want to be able to read them their bedtime stories without frightening obsessive thoughts racing through my mind. With recovery, I could be a better wife and mom to the most important people in my life. I know God wants me to work at this Twelve-Step program, and to get whatever help I need, medical or otherwise, in order to be healthier.

I can say at this early stage that our program is starting to help me achieve some measure of serenity – something I've so desperately wanted in my life. I find myself with a greater acceptance of people and circumstances over which I have no control. Feeling of frustration and anxieties are being replaced with a greater peace of mind. I think this is because I trust in my Higher Power, God, and his will for me. I'll always be a member of OCA – it's there that I belong.

(10)
A Painful Struggle

I have had OCD for as long as I can remember. My teen years were very difficult because that's when my OCD really became obvious to me. I began checking and rechecking certain things. I also started a pattern of repeating things four times.

Growing up I knew that there was something wrong, but I was always able to live with the strange things that I did. Up until last year, as time went on, nothing changed. My two main problems continue to be my repeating and my constant checking. I have some days that are fine but there are other days when my OCD rituals feel unbearable. My feelings about myself are very low and I feel that I do everything wrong.

I am constantly checking such things as the car door to assure that the light is off when I close the door, or my alarm clock to guarantee that it is set correctly for the next day. I could go on and on describing my ritualistic behaviors. Once I start checking I can't do anything to control myself; I become obsessed with these rituals.

I have learned that I cannot fight OCD alone. Once I get started, there is no turning back. I feel that I must complete my ritual.

I also feel compelled to repeat things. I am constantly repeating things to my wife, but manage to say the same thing again using different words if she becomes annoyed.

Through the years I have been to two psychiatrists. Although at the time I was sure that I was having a heart attack, I was also hospitalized for what turned out to be an anxiety attack.

One year ago I joined a 12-step program for OCD, which I've been attending once a week ever since. Although I still have my compulsions, and I don't believe that I'll ever be totally cured of OCD, I feel that the meetings have helped reduce the rituals.

It's wonderful to be able to talk to people with similar problems without feeling embarrassed. I have met some very nice people in the rooms who suffer the same pain as I do. The meeting gives us an opportunity to get together and share with each other what we are going through.

I have recently started taking anti-obsessional medication to combat some of the OCD symptoms. Although I have avoided using medications throughout the years, I now feel that the combination of the 12 step program and this medication offers me a greater opportunity to enjoy things more and live a happier life.

(11)
A Simple Letter?

What a wonderful time my girlfriend and I had last night! I love her very much. The next day I found a love letter in the mailbox from her. It was a nice surprise – until I had what I call a "thought attack." My mind began to race with fear: "I must contact her to express my gratitude for the letter"..."What if I say something wrong?"... "My voice may crack or the inflection of my words may be inappropriate"... "I just know I'm going to ruin this beautiful relationship I've found"...

Finally, through careful (and I mean careful in the most agonizing sense of the word) thought, I come up with an idea. I'll send her a letter and postscript it with "I'll call you tomorrow, Sweetie." This will buy me some time. I write the letter. The process is emotionally exhausting. I have to read the letter over and over again, until I am sure I have not written anything inappropriate, hurtful, or destructive to the relationship. Although I have read it no less than fifteen times, I still have many doubts about what I have written. I still don't know whether I have written something that will ruin my new relationship. My doubting is my disease. I feel like crying.

Finally, I leave for my girlfriend's house. I have to make sure she is not home. After calling and getting no answer, I drive over. I am afraid I will drive by her on the road and then my great plan will collapse. I'm afraid if I run into her, I will say something inappropriate and lose her. The drive over is agonizing. I'm filled with anxiety. I pull onto her street, terrified that I will meet her there, but I don't. I run out of my car and place the letter sticking out of the mailbox. It takes a minute just to make sure it is positioned correctly.

I leave, and get about three quarters of a mile away, when I become terrified that the postscript on the back of the envelope is not, "I'll call you tomorrow, sweetie," but something sick, inappropriate, perverse, or just plain crazy. I just don't know. I doubt and doubt. I drive back, read it over and over till I am convinced that all is well, and then go home. No sooner do I get home then I begin to doubt all that is written in the letter. Have I blown it? Did I write something inappropriate? My sleep is restless and terror-filled. I feel like my mind is torturing me. Please God, help me.

The next day I call her and discover she is sick. She doesn't fawn over me, and I become terrified that I have written something sick and distorted. I am exhausted.

That night I see her and, once again, she declares her love for me. The whole maze of worry I went through was groundless. Why does this go on? I am tortured by my own mind.

Meanwhile, all the time this has been going on I have also been counting and checking, compulsively closing the car door TWICE (it must be twice!). I check the car lights over and over again, touching the steering wheel twice, looking at the traffic light or a passerby twice. The counting and checking goes on as a background to my daily life, and even to the incident I have just described about my girlfriend. The process is a true nightmare, and I feel quite powerless to stop it all. If I try to stop my behavior, I get tremendous rushes of anxiety and fear.

Now I am in OCA and am also receiving medical attention. I have great hope that I will recover from this Obsessive Compulsive Disorder, and live in peace and joy with the woman I love. I know that without recovery I don't stand a chance. I am very relieved to have found Obsessive Compulsive Anonymous. I have great hope now!

(12)
My Own Private Hell

I don't know what the day or the date was, or the actual situation that had occurred. I do know that I had the feeling that something was not right; that I wasn't "quite right," – this feeling would stay with me for over ten years. I was a "picker." This might sound dumb, but it's true. I picked on myself by picking at my skin. Although most commonly at my face, I picked at whatever I thought didn't belong on any parts of my body. You see, I wanted to be perfect. I simply would not stand for having blemishes or flaws on myself, so the only thing for me to do was to get rid of them. This made perfect sense to me at the time, but after a while I realized that I couldn't stop. My favorite room in the house became the bathroom. I spent hours in there – just me, myself, and the soooo-dreaded mirror.

I examined myself intensely, not because I liked to but because I had to. Naturally, by the time I was finished that part of my body that I picked (usually my face) was totally red. I fooled everyone ... except myself. When my mom asked, "What happened to your face?" I said that I was using a new face scrub or that I had used too much hot water, etc, etc.

I had all of the answers, except for why I was doing this outrageous crime to myself. I hadn't yet known about OCD. I only knew that when the picking started to get worse (such as my using pins and needles to dig at my skin) I needed help.

Once diagnosed as having OCD, my therapist exposed me to Obsessive Compulsive Anonymous (OCA). It was there that I met a group of people who shared a common disorder – the recurrence of obsessions and compulsions – and a common goal – to work together to make life more bearable.

It was recommended to me to buy the Alcoholics Anonymous (A.A.) book, *The Twelve Steps and Twelve Traditions.* I was told to substitute the word "alcohol" with the term "OCD," and to apply the steps to my own particular problem. I've gotten through half of the twelve steps but I need to go back and rework them.

Although I'm new in OCA, the Program has started to help me. Perhaps more helpful to me than the book has been the people in the OCA group. They are the ones who come each week to share their stories and offer bits of helpful suggestions. I am grateful to each one of these individuals.

Perhaps one day I'll start a group or try to reach out to someone else who is struggling with OCD. But, in the meantime, I'll stick to learning the twelve steps and attending weekly OCA meetings. At the very least, I know that I'm not alone. My own private hell isn't just mine. For once, it felt good to open up and tell other people that I've got this problem – this insane urge to hurt myself. It helps to know that there are people who understand and have gone the same route as I have.

Maybe someone who is reading this will identify with it. I hope not, for no one should go through the pain, but if you do, it's important to recognize that this problem is not unique. There are others who are suffering with it and who know about the pain and the guilt that you have. Above all, it's not your fault. For me that was reassuring.

It's up to me, and you, though, to do something about it. Since it's true that there's "strength in numbers," we can work together to help each other battle this disease. The worst thing is thinking that you're the only one suffering with these compulsions and/or obsessions. Thank God, though, we know that this is not true. We are not alone.

(13)
Haunted By Fears

Writing this story is one of the most difficult, and yet one of the most beneficial things I've been asked to do. The difficulty, as well as the benefits arise from the necessity to truly confront the reality of my Obsessive Compulsive Disorder (OCD) and how it has affected my entire life. Within this past year (1989) I've actually become painfully aware that I have OCD. I can safely say that I have spent at least the last twenty-four years cowering to the whims of my OCD. I never stopped to consider that my behavior might have been somewhat bizarre, although I knew, even as a young child, that I was motivated to perform obsessive rituals solely on the basis of my fear ... but fear of what, of whom? I had a vague sense that "something" mystical and animated, or "someone" cruel and hostile would "get me;" I performed strange behaviors to ward off the tragic outcomes I feared. I checked closets, underneath beds, outside second-floor windows, and anywhere else I may have contrived that these creatures or bogie-men could be hiding.

Although there was a great deal of unexpressed love and (somewhat overbearing) concern in my family, my home was noticeably filled with tension and fear. As the third and youngest of three daughters, I became abnormally dependent on my mother and emulated most of her fears while I silently created a plethora of my own.

I realize now that "magical thinking" has been associated with almost every action I've taken throughout my life. It would be fruitless to even begin to describe the barrage of obsessions and complementary rituals I have experienced. Suffice it to say that there have been plenty, ranging from the terror and panic ignited by not knowing how an object got lost or moved, to the need to say special prayers, or to say specific words a precise number of times.

As an easily impressionable teenager with a compulsive personality, I spent much of my high school and college days excessively drinking alcohol and abusing drugs. What I called "partying" was actually a means of covering up my feelings and avoiding reality. In many ways I believe my OCD has served, and often continues to serve, the same purpose. As I reflect back, I can see that it was quite a "trip" being incredibly high on drugs and drunk on whiskey while obsessing about how an object was moved, and performing rituals to avoid contact with that object. I also began bingeing and vomiting in college, and remained bulimic for the next five years. I now see that almost every time I began a cycle of bingeing and purging I had eaten foods which my distorted thinking deemed as "jinxed" or "spooky" and therefore too harmful to remain in my body. It floors me to think of how insidious and destructive OCD can actually be.

As I let go of my bulimic behavior and my drug and alcohol abuse (from fear of eventually killing myself), I latched on to anorexia, with which I have been struggling ever since. Although it has taken on several different forms throughout the years, OCD has accompanied all of my various addictions and self-destructive actions.

I know today that I can't change what I have done, but I can affect what actions I take now. In 1982, when I stopped drinking alcohol and abusing drugs, I was fortunate enough to frequent many open Alcoholics Anonymous (A.A.) meetings and bear witness to the miracles of recovery. Since my eating disorder was my primary problem, I eventually became a member of Overeaters Anonymous (OA).

The Twelve-Step Program has given me an opportunity to grow, emotionally and spiritually. As I apply the Program's principles to all areas of my life, I can actually see the process of recovery taking place. Although I'd been in OA (as well as psychotherapy) for over seven years it wasn't until this past year that I learned I have a disease believed to be caused by a biochemical imbalance. Until recently, I believed that my thoughts and behaviors were so bizarre that no one would understand them (especially since I didn't truly understand the nature of these obsessions and rituals myself). I tried to hide them and appear as normal as I possibly could. Needless to say, eventually family and friends did notice my strange actions, but either joked about them or denied that I could actually be behaving in such a strange manner. It wasn't until I accidentally slipped to my therapist about my "insane thoughts" that I learned that other people also suffer with obsessions and compulsions that they too feel powerless over.

After several months of strong denial, I finally surrendered to the reality that I had a disease which required as much, if not more, treatment than my eating disorder and other addictive behaviors. Following months of paralyzing anxiety attacks, I sought help from a behavior therapist who specializes in treating people with OCD. I began the flooding process which required me to directly and honestly confront my fears and refrain from performing rituals to counteract "potential doom."

The agony of OCD was so great that I thought I was willing to go to any lengths to lessen the pain and live my life more sanely. I mistakenly thought I had surrendered to the process of recovery, but soon learned that my fear-based willfulness to remain governed by the OCD was stronger than I had ever imagined. Eventually, however, because my life was so unmanageable, I began to risk challenging my unfounded fears and beliefs.

Tackling OCD has been the hardest endeavor I've ever attempted. However, as I continue the process of facing my fears, I find my life becoming a bit more sane and my abilities revitalizing. Additionally, although I was initially quite opposed to taking medication, I have recently begun incorporating it into my recovery program.

By questioning and confronting my obsessive fears and their corresponding rituals, I have accomplished feats that I never thought possible. I know, though, that I could never have accomplished any of these things had I not trusted in the tools of the Twelve-Step Program to guide me.

As I began allowing myself to be humble about having the disease, I started selectively confiding in a few close program friends. Although I rationally understood that OCD is a biochemical disorder over which I am completely powerless by myself, emotionally I believed that I was quite deranged for having such strange thoughts and performing such bizarre rituals. Therefore, it was quite a risk for me to divulge my darkest secret, even to these friends, who knew more about me than many of my own family members.

Humbled by the pain of obsessing and ritualizing, I let go of the fear of judgment and rejection and gathered a haven of supportive people to help me along the path of recovery. Sharing my trepidation and terror with understanding program friends before and after I abstained from performing a ritual took some of the power away from the disease; I felt more comforted, and even proud of myself. I also use the tool of writing to release my negative feelings and paralyzing fears. This helps me to quiet the chatter in my mind and alleviate the anxiety created by my OCD.

The support I received from knowledgeable and caring professionals, as well as family and friends, has encouraged me to continue my trek. I have found that speaking with others who have OCD has helped me tremendously and has enabled me to be more honest about my disease.

As I tackle some difficult OCD-related fears, the life-issues which these fears have masked for so many years are now surfacing, requiring me to acknowledge and deal with them. Although often terrifying, this has been an exciting and exhilarating process. I've also noticed that the path of recovery is not straight and smooth, but sometimes extremely bumpy.

As I have begun acting in a healthier manner I've noticed that the OCD is holding on, desperately trying to maintain its place in my life. I find this frustrating, but I am also grateful to have insight and awareness about it which I never had before.

I experience anger toward my obsessions and rituals because I truly want to live my life more fully without being robbed by this disease. Although I do not believe that I will ever be totally rid of the obsessions, I know that through perseverance, honesty and a willingness to work the Twelve-Step Program, my life can be fuller and more rewarding. I am extremely grateful to all those people who continue to stand by me and help me on my journey of recovery.

(14)
A Living Hell

The title of this story may sound dramatic to most readers, but it probably seems quite accurate to a person who has OCD.

I guess you would say that I'm a "checker" since that seems the most fitting label for my symptoms. I remember spending a lot of time as a child moving objects in my room and counting each time I moved something. There was no way I could leave my house for school unless I closed my dresser drawer a certain way and counted while doing that. Of course, this ritual varied from object to object and number to number.

As I got older, the checking of objects seemed to change to the checking of my own thoughts. Sometimes I thought about things people had said or experiences that I had and counted how many times I thought about them. While I was counting, a tremendous feeling of guilt and depression overcame me. I didn't know why this was happening but it just seemed impossible not to obsess.

When I became fourteen years old I started coming out of it. I made some new friends and things seemed to be looking up for me. My friends and I experimented with drugs and I found out quickly that drugs and OCD don't mix very well. The drugs made me feel important – like one of the guys.

I was always ready to go out with this group and try something new. One night we were experimenting. I wanted to show how "macho" I was so I took a double dose of what everyone else was taking. The next twelve hours were pure hell. When the drug wore off, I thought I had learned my vicious lesson, but the trouble was just beginning for me.

I began obsessing about this experience twenty-four hours

a day, seven days a week. I was no longer able to go to the places that reminded me of that bad experience. However, the problem was that these places included my own house, my friends' houses, and practically everything in my neighborhood. I began eliminating each place and activity one by one because I feared each one so greatly. When I was around these stimuli I began to sweat, my heart raced, my ears rang, and my vision blurred. In the midst of what I later learned is called a panic attack, I lived and relived every day (sometimes four times daily) the feeling that I was going to die. This went on for the next fourteen years.

I consulted ear and eye doctors, practiced meditation, and read various self-help books. I learned a lot from a psychologist who I was seeing for four years but I was still obsessive and compulsive. Like most people stricken with a relentless depression, I considered suicide but that was too scary.

By that point I realized that I had virtually tried everything to relieve my torture. One day, as I was looking through a magazine for something to help me, I found an article about Obsessive Compulsive Anonymous (OCA). After attending my first meeting a tremendous weight was lifted from my shoulders. There were people at that meeting who understood what I was saying. For the first time in fourteen years I heard other people speaking about the same struggles I had experienced.

It was very difficult to speak in front of a group of people about something that had been a dark secret filled with fear and anxiety for so long. Looking out at the group though, I saw friendly, understanding faces. At that point I knew I had a chance.

By combining medication with my OCA meetings, I've experienced a good percentage of recovery and I've rediscovered serenity. With the help of my OCA friends I'm living a much fuller life now. I used to think that I wouldn't have a family, but I've been blessed with a beautiful, supportive wife and a son.

Every once in a while I think about my father who passed away engulfed in the horrors of OCD. He never had a chance since he never really knew what he had. I also think about the other people who are suffering with OCD unaware, and I pray that God will give them some direction.

(15)
Coming Home to OCA

I am thirty-three years old and I have had OCD for nineteen years. I remember it latched onto me and I became a completely different person. When I was fifteen years old I had a conversation with my best friend. I told her it felt like I finally got control over my life because I invented this new thing that I could do to make myself feel better. She asked me what it was and I told her that I was making lists of everything that was going on in my mind all of the time. She did not understand why this was so wonderful. She thought it was weird and she was concerned for me. I realized I was doing something that nobody else was doing. Because of her reaction I never told anyone again. I knew that ultimately I did not want to do it, but it was a desperate attempt to manage a life that felt like hell. I felt a desperate loss of my natural self. I felt like I was no longer really alive. I knew that there was nothing wonderful about my list; it was just a way to survive hell.

Next, my obsessive thoughts became so intense that no amount of list writing could control them. I had thoughts all of the time then – when I talked to a friend my brain was split and I thought I was going crazy. I was also anorectic – severely anorectic. I almost died from it. I was obsessed with counting calories and running up and down the stairs to burn off a piece of cake. I performed many rituals around this until I finally overcame the anorexia – out of the blue I just decided to eat. I suddenly realized that if I did not eat very soon – that day – I was going to die because I was so thin.

I was so tortured by thoughts that there were years when I did not sleep at night except when I drank myself into a blackout. I wrote in journals constantly, I had a suitcase full of journals. I could not concentrate on anything. In college I often stayed up all night because there were times when it took me seven hours to get through seven pages of a book. Sometimes in class I felt my brain clench like a fist. I felt like I was about to go stark-raving insane, but I was so afraid that everyone would find out I was crazy that I continued to take notes while I was actually freaking out inside. I was so concerned about appearing normal. I felt like there was no one I could talk to about this. Instead, I said silently over and over to myself, " I am not going to go insane – I am not going to go insane."

The scariest episode that happened during the time of this obsessive nightmare was when I went up to the top of a popular lookout point on the Oregon coast with the man I later married. It was a very high cliff without a fence surrounding it. At that point in my life I really couldn't do anything – I could not dance, I could not walk, I could not talk – the thoughts accompanied me all the time and kept me from being spontaneous. I had horrible dreams at night if I slept. I felt like I was possessed by a thousand demons and there I was up on this cliff without a fence.

Meanwhile, my fiancé was on the other edge taking pictures of whales and other people were sitting with their behinds half off the cliff's edge. I felt so out of control and possessed by my own mind because this dark part of me asked, "What do you have to live for? You cannot read anymore, you cannot laugh anymore – everything is death to you. Sure, as a child you enjoyed life immensely, but now it is all gone."

It was true. I felt like I was buried alive, like I was already dead. The dark part of me said, "You have no reason to live. Why don't you just fling yourself off the cliff and end it all?" So I clung to a pole. Thank God the pole was there! I prayed some Jewish prayers over and over again and they saved me. I was praying like I was going to fall apart at the seams; I prayed until I felt I could no longer pray. At that point my fiancé turned to me and said, "Let's go back down," not knowing what I had been through.

One of the main aspects of my OCD was never telling anyone what I was going through. I felt like I would be put away in an asylum if people knew what I was really like.

I am now working on looking back to see the sources of my OCD. These are some of the things I have learned: I grew up in a family where it was never O.K. to say "NO"– never O.K. to express my feelings. Therefore, I had to depend on myself for emotional support because there was no one to whom I could go. I was the eldest of four children. I realize that OCD is the disease of playing God and trying to control everything. I did not understand the concepts of letting go or depending on someone besides myself. The relationships I had as an adult were very much the same as those I had while growing up – violent and abusive. To me, family meant people I had to defend myself against, people upon whom I could not depend, people around whom I lived a secret life.

As a child I was molested several times by male and female perpetrators. When I grew up I felt that sex, when it was not performed as a form of rape, was something to be endured. My OCD was wrapped up in protecting me when it came to sex. It was a way to avoid contacting the profound pain I went through. I was thirty years old before I realized, "Hey, I don't have to do this anymore. I don't have to be in violent relationships, don't have to have sex when I don't like it." I believe that abuse and OCD are intrinsically linked: Repressing the sexual abuse memories was one of the key reasons I drank and developed OCD and anorexia. Although I have made vast improvements, I still have not experienced my sexuality. I have had glimmers and I am getting better, but I am in my thirties and feel that I am twelve or thirteen years old in my sexual development.

Now I will describe my experience, strength and hope. I will start with how I got into OCA. Three years ago I joined A.A. I have always had a mustard seed of faith. It was a very tiny, tiny mustard seed – the size of an atom – that said if I somehow believe there is a God, I will get beyond this. One of the roots of my alcoholism was OCD. Having even one black-out provided me peace from my obsessional thoughts. Once I began studying the Twelve Steps I latched onto Step Two, a belief in a power greater than myself.

I felt like I was starting completely from scratch when I joined A.A. Something changed – a miracle arrived – there was something intangible about it. Although it had to do with the fellowship, the sharing, the laughter and a belief in a Higher Power, it was something beyond that. Yet I knew something else was missing. Something was still not right. Although I wasn't drinking (I know I would have killed myself with alcohol), before I found OCA my thoughts were still possessing me like demons. I was desperate! I did not know what to do. I had tried so many things during those eight years, including religion, consulting tarot cards, and meditation, but nothing lifted this merciless obsession from me. "God, there has to be someone else like me," I hoped. Basically though, I figured I was the only person and thought, "God, how can I be so weird?" That thought made it even worse. I felt like, "Why am I on this planet? Why am I here? I am not even living anymore. I stopped living when I was fourteen."

In May of 1990 I discovered the book *The Boy Who Couldn't Stop Washing.* I pulled it off the shelf, started reading and saw right away that that's what I had. I couldn't believe it; I had Obsessive Compulsive Disorder. It had a name. There were other people who also had it. I was completely blown away. So I sought out and found a hospital with a treatment program for OCD sufferers. I participated in behavior therapy and was treated with medication. Although this treatment helped a great deal, I knew from the beginning that it was not the complete answer.

Once I realized what I did have, I started thinking hard about starting a Twelve Step group for OCD sufferers. I knew my OCD had to do with my whole way of being in the world – it wasn't just a chemical. I decided to start a Twelve Step group to address OCD and discovered that someone had already started one. I called its founder and got things going. Part of me was relieved that this was going to be easy. Taking the easy way has been hard for me too. I feel more at home when things are difficult. I had to learn to keep it simple – to follow the saying "Easy does it." Many, many people helped me start this group. The first San Francisco group was born precisely because so many people in OCA were so very helpful.

My life has changed tremendously. The freedom growing in me toward peace of mind is truly a miracle. Recovery from OCD means living again, and in the process looking at how I live and relate to others, to myself and to God. My OCD highlights for me how I handle life – its challenges and the feelings that come up. One of the most powerful lessons I have received from OCA is to put my hand in someone else's to help each other and reach out. I learned how to have relationships as well as true feelings. I now tell people what is really going on inside of me. There are even a few people at work, and of course my partner, who truly know what is going on inside. Now when I have OCD episodes I consider them opportunities because they spark me into going to meetings, reading the A.A. Big Book, reaching out to other people to be helped or to help those people who are suffering more than I am. I've learned in OCA that my recovery is not in my hands. It is in my feet because I do the footwork. Ultimately though, I leave the rest to God.

After three years of Twelve Step work I finally understand the Serenity Prayer. Finally I understand that it means asking for the serenity to accept and change the things I can, doing the footwork but realizing that God will take care of the rest. The rest will get resolved. I realize I have to give it time; there aren't any easy solutions – there is just one day at a time and living the Twelve Steps.

I also realized that my OCD was a disease of extreme self-centeredness. I was constantly wrapped up in my problems, always thinking about them and performing rituals. I have seen that recovery from OCD means reaching out to other people, thinking about their needs and calling them. More than in any other program I have found that SERVICE in OCA keeps me ABSTINENT from my OCD behaviors. When I am suffering through an OCD episode it is so HEALING to call someone and see how that person is doing. There are people who cannot make it to an OCA meeting because OCD keeps them in their homes.

One of the most helpful prayers from A.A. that I say to myself is the Third Step prayer. I feel so grateful that I can say that and mean it. I used to think, "But I want my way; I want to have a great time and I do not want to turn it over to God because I will probably end up doing things that aren't any fun." But I found out that turning it over to God means that I have a life far beyond what I could have conceived of myself .

Besides my wonderful fellowship of OCA, I believe in relaxing a lot, which is something I never did before. I also just let myself be taken care of by letting other people reach in to help. Just letting go and letting God work through other people is a real struggle for me.

Now, for the most part I do not suffer from OCD at all. Sometimes OCD episodes arise when I make changes, move to a new place or when feelings come up. OCD is a way of saying, "Whoa, there is something very heavy going on here." I know I have many years of healing ahead of me, but for the most part I can make friends, I can do my work and keep my job and I can experience peace of mind.

It is such a special miracle that there is nothing more important than my OCA fellowship and working on the Twelve Steps of OCA. I feel that my work in OCA is my greatest purpose in life and the thing I love the most. I am really lucky because in addition to OCA I have a partner who, even though she does not have OCD, is really able to learn as much as she can, hear me, understand and offer me deep compassion. Being heard and understood are vital and are things many of us did not have, and may have greatly contributed to why we have OCD. When I go to OCA meetings I know I am home – home in a way I have never been before. I am very grateful for OCA and I am very grateful for this opportunity to tell my story. THANK YOU!

(16)
My Life

I believe that I have had OCD throughout my life. It has affected my self-esteem and made me feel insecure around other people.

Growing up I recall having to constantly check things over and over. Many times I would excessively check to make sure I locked the front door at my parents' home. Also, I'd wash my hands for a long period of time to alleviate the obsession that they were still contaminated. The simple tasks in life became difficult to accomplish whenever I was preoccupied with my OCD thoughts.

My work habits were affected each time I held a job. While working as a bank teller, I used to see my OCD frequently interfere with my normal routine. For instance, I would spend a long time just counting the money received from the customer. Also, I would constantly doubt my ability to make decisions on the job. I would compulsively ask questions of my coworkers. Many times I would hold up the line of customers for fifteen to thirty minutes while I went about the bank to find an answer to my particular problem.

Before I attended OCA I was a silent sufferer. Essentially I covered up my feelings so that no one would know I had a problem. As a result I was distant toward people and spent most of the time caught up in my own thoughts. I developed a poor self-image and became used to wallowing in self-pity.

My parents wanted to help but couldn't understand how troubled I was. Many times I'd be stuck in the bathroom washing my hands and my parents wanted me to stop. But it wasn't that easy, the OCD had affected me deeply.

Being a member of OCA, I've become aware that I'm not

the only one with the rituals. Furthermore, the group addresses the fact that we can feel better by getting active in our own
recovery. Through OCA I've learned to accept my past and
grow from it. I understand more about the disorder by attending meetings and relating to people who have OCD. In
addition, I try to go easy on myself and not blame myself for
having it.

At OCA I have slowly been able to enjoy peace of mind
and feel better about myself. I embrace the notion of a Higher
Power and feel glad knowing that he can relieve my obsessions
and compulsions whenever I'm doing His will. As long as I
keep an open mind and have a desire to help others, I know I'll
continue to enjoy recovery.

I feel I have changed my life for the better, now that I have
gotten involved with OCA and the Twelve Step process. I have
held leadership positions in the group and this has enhanced
my recovery. I truly am grateful to my Higher Power and the
members of OCA who have given me support and guidance
throughout the years.

(17)
Worry's My Name,
Control's My Game

For as long as I can remember, I've been a worrier. I guess I first began worrying about my father, who had a serious chronic illness since the time I was an infant. My worrying wasn't a daily routine – it happened intermittently. Yet, I recall that it was extremely obsessive and consuming. Besides his health, I also worried about my dad's drinking, which became excessive when I was twelve years old.

I excelled in school and found a great deal of gratification in running track and playing on the high school basketball team. Externally I looked good, but internally I carried much fear and insecurity. In the secrecy of my own mind I worried about numerous things, many of which I shared with no one.

In my mid-twenties I was thrown into a serious obsessive episode because of a break-up with a girlfriend. I blamed myself for the break-up even though she left me. I played our relationship over and over in my mind as a perfectionist football quarterback might mentally replay the Sunday game films on Monday morning, relentlessly trying to ferret out the flaws that resulted in losing the game. It wasn't until much later in my life that I realized how my response to the separation was a "safe" way for me to control the rage I felt at being abandoned.

I became obsessed with my health and with fears of contamination. I worried that I would get cancer from environmental toxins and I feared I might get AIDS from handshakes, food or doorknobs. The anxious preoccupations were not based on reality. I had no obvious symptoms nor was I at risk for AIDS, yet I created "what if" scenarios in my mind, imagining that something horrible was surely going to happen to me. There were many days when I found it next to impossible to focus on anything else. To get relief I called the EPA or other healthcare professionals. Sometimes I would even visit my doctor. The reassurance they gave me was usually short-lived and the worries returned. I felt like I was becoming a "reassurance junkie." My compulsions to get reassurance were extremely compelling. I feel these compulsions affected my family and my work. Even now, when I look at my life I see how I obsessively worry about so many (usually petty) things.

Five months ago, my wife, who is a social worker, came home from her job and showed me a pamphlet about OCD. I read it with much interest. I'd heard about obsessive-compulsive behavior while I was attending graduate school, and even joked with my roommate about how we both fit the profile. I later took it very seriously because my pattern of worrying was getting way out of hand. That pamphlet about OCD opened a door for me. There was a name for what I was experiencing. Others struggle with the same thing. I wrote to the OC Foundation for additional materials and I also learned about OCA. I spoke with someone in a local group and attended a meeting. I also consulted a psychiatrist who believed that I was experiencing OCD.

At first I thought that "knowing" about OCD would enable me to control it ... wrong! My symptoms continued. About two months ago, after attending an OCA meeting on Step Three, I told a group member about the struggle I was having in "letting go" of my worries. He said, "That's right, you can't let go on your own; you need to ask for help." That night I began to ask God to help me let go of my obsessive worries. I've never really doubted the existence of God. While I had known about the Twelve Steps through Adult Children of Alcoholics, I'd never really worked Step Three as I do now. I resisted turning my life and my will over to God, not because I doubted God's existence, but because I didn't want to let go of the reins. As painful as my worry-filled life became, I didn't want to let go of my control game.

Knowing about and doing the Third Step has brought new serenity into my life. I still have my obsessive days, but they are not as powerful as they had been before. I have friends who know my struggle and I have tools to cope.

OCA is not the only support I've utilized. I've also been in therapy for the past two years. Through this process I've been able to name some of my anxieties – such as my ambivalence about being a parent and my fears about working through my marriage conflicts. I've now come to view my OCD as a merry-go-round out of control. When I want to avoid feeling something such as hurt or anger (it may even be a positive feeling such as joy), I begin to worry so that I won't feel it. Identifying and expressing feelings has always been a challenge for me and I certainly relate to the ACOA litany, "don't talk, don't trust, don't feel." At the same time I am open to the possibility that there is something biochemical that perpetuates my merry-go-round of worry. Still, I sincerely believe that it's my need to control emotions that starts the merry-go-round.

When I'm working hard to be in control the question "What if .... ?" spins a web around my mind. What if I've been contaminated by this or that? What if? What if? I ask "What if ... ?" in order to gain control, but that same "What if ... ?" has brought me to my knees, powerless and feeling very much out of control. There was a point at which I was ready to try medication but decided not to when I began experiencing some relief from my symptoms by attending OCA meetings, working the steps and using other Twelve Step tools such as the telephone.

OCA is a key part of my recovery process. When I began

attending meetings I wanted to "destroy" my obsessiveness. I hated how I worried throughout my life and I just wanted to get rid of that characteristic. I've come now to see my worrying not only as an addiction to my need to be in control, but also as an opportunity to get more healing into my life. I see it now as a signal to pay more attention to my feelings and my needs for support. I haven't learned to love my obsession to worry, but slowly I've learned through the fellowship how to make friends with it.

Humor is very important to my recovery. While the following prayer I wrote is not really humorous (especially when one has lived the prayer for such a long time), I can actually smile now as I read it.

Control Prayer
God, give me the power to control the things I cannot (control)
the fear to avoid the things I can (control)
and the foolishness to think there's much difference

Thanks to the Twelve Step program I now know of another prayer which expresses a better way to live – the Serenity Prayer. It feels very risky to "live life on life's terms" and to live "one day at a time" – it's a way of living that I'm not used to – it's a way of living that provides me more freedom from OCD.

(18)
A Clearer Picture

Every person has many sides. One of mine is that I am a commercial artist. In the over twenty years that I have been in this field I have been fairly successful, but I had difficulties being productive. I sometimes also had difficulties finding peace of mind and personal fulfillment due to depression and perfectionism. Eventually I developed OCD. The more I fought against this illness by myself, the worse it got. It wasted more and more of my time and energy and made my existence more and more miserable.

Then one day I admitted that I needed outside help with all these problems. I sought help both professionally and with the Twelve Step fellowships. Thanks to my faith in God as I understand Him and the assistance of the program, I am now on a path of recovery and personal growth, which has changed my life for the better.

One of the things which has brought joy and recognition to me in my life has been my artistic talent. I have been drawing pictures since I was four years old. This impressed adults, especially my mother who would proudly show off my work to friends and relatives. When I entered elementary school I dazzled my teachers and classmates with how well and how fast I drew. It is ironic to me that after I grew up and became a commercial artist that my perfectionism would cause me to acquire a reputation for working slowly.

I come from a Latino background and grew up in New York City with my mother, father, my older brother and two younger sisters. My youngest sister, unfortunately, was born with mental retardation and has had to have all her needs taken care of by someone else.

My first bout with mental illness was with clinical depression. When I was eleven years old, I experienced an episode that lasted an entire month. One day I was a happy schoolboy and the next I was continually sad. I would weep uncontrollably at any time and everything in my life seemed to have lost all meaning. At least I had an idea of what my problem was, though. I read a comic strip where one of the characters often went through depressions and I identified with him. I have gone through several more episodes of depression since then. The next year my mother and father were legally separated after a big fight. There was occasionally tension in our home over the years because of how my father acted when he got drunk. Sometimes he would go out on a Friday night and we wouldn't know at what time he would come home or what would happen when he did. Sometimes he'd have a loud fight with mom. These scenes made me feel anxious and sad.

After I graduated from junior high school I went to one of the special high schools in New York. This one was for art and music students. It was considered a notable achievement to be accepted there. However, for me it was sometimes a lonely and isolating experience. I was shy and felt intimidated by the sophistication and outspokenness of some of the other students. I wound up having only a few friends, but I got good grades and earned my diploma.

I then went to community college where I studied commercial art. The course of study was a lot of work, but I got good grades there as well and earned a degree.

Right out of school I got a job at the corporate headquarters of a major department store chain. Being able to work quickly is valued in the commercial art field because an important part of the business is meeting deadlines and schedules. Due to my perfectionism I had a hard time doing this. However the quality of my work won me a promotion after three years.

I was my boss's assistant. My job was to prepare the copy for the signs that the board artists would assemble. My perfectionism made me fall behind in my work. I was supposed to be an executive but I didn't know to act. I felt isolated from the other employees. I often worked long hours and sometimes left the office late at night when only the cleaning people were there. I started to get stomach cramps. I hated it. After a year I quit.

After I left, I got a job on staff at a comic book company doing lettering corrections on the pages before they were sent to the printer. I was overjoyed. I had always wanted to be a cartoonist since before I knew how to read and now I finally had the chance to break into the field. Over the next six years I did different types of work, including writing and drawing joke pages. Eventually I became a freelancer in order to draw a new comic book (which I helped create) on a regular basis.

It was at this point that my perfectionism and depression were joined by OCD. I started to take longer to get things done. I would draw and redraw figures on the page until there was an impression, almost like an embossment on the other side of the paper. I would procrastinate about getting started every day because I felt anxious or lonely or resentful. I would go over and over in my mind the hurts or insults others had done to me. I felt frustrated because I couldn't meet my deadlines. The work I had always wanted to do since I was a child was turning into an ordeal.

Eventually the comic book I was drawing was canceled because of dropping sales. I wasn't able to get enough new work drawing as a freelancer, so I took a staff job at the comic book company. Once again I was doing lettering corrections and lettering copy for the covers. The OCD also continued to get worse. I had contamination fears. I would constantly wash my hands until the skin turned red and cracked. If I dropped a tool on the floor I had to wash it. My work would pile up undone. I once spent an entire day drawing and redrawing one letter "E". I started staying late again, sometimes until about midnight. Some of my fellow workers, noticing my behavior, would make jokes about me.

I would come in late to work most days, sometimes by an hour or more. It took me an hour just to take a shower. I would check the sliding door of the shower stall over and over. I feared it would come off the tracks and hurt someone. Magazines from subscriptions would pile up unread. So would junk mail. I could only throw it out if I had read it. I felt that if I didn't read all of the solicitations from all the different charities I was being a mean person. And reading took more and more time. I would read sentences and paragraphs over and over if I didn't understand them perfectly or missed even a comma. I felt as if I was losing my mind.

Yet, in the middle of this distress, there was hope and progress. I like to listen to the radio. I love music, but I also like interesting talk shows. One day I heard an interview show. The guest seemed to be a psychologist. She mentioned a list of traits that are common among adult children of alcoholics. I identified with the list. I realized that I was an ACOA and that I was not alone. I started to read books about ACOAs and subscribed to a recovery magazine.

Later I heard Suzanne Somers on the radio talking about her experiences as an ACOA. She mentioned how she had met a sympathetic psychologist who charged her only five dollars a session because she was short on funds at the time. This encouraged me and a year later I finally worked up the nerve to seek out a therapist for myself. She was also sympathetic and charged me only half price. At the age of thirty-four I was finally getting treatment for my depression and low self-esteem.

A few months later, after having read about other peoples' experiences, I went to my first Twelve Step meeting for ACOAs. This meeting was part of Al-Anon, which is the fellowship for friends and relatives of alcoholics. I also began to attend a general Al-Anon meeting as well as another meeting specifically for ACOAs. With the help of these fellowships, my problems started to improve, including my OCD.

Although I was making progress with my problems in general, I was still having trouble with OCD. I was still not as productive as I needed to be at work. Then the OCD started getting worse and I went into a bad depression. At this point my therapist sent me to a psychiatrist. She diagnosed me as having OCD and prescribed a medication which is widely used for it. I had seen OCD described in an episode of *Innovation* on Public Television and in a segment on the program 20/20. I realized I had many of the same symptoms that the sufferers portrayed in these reports did.

I had been avoiding using medications since I had started therapy. It is my personal feeling that the more you can recover without them the better. However, in this instance I needed a boost to get me out of the funk I was in. After two months on the medication, my symptoms were substantially relieved. But I had exhausted my employer's patience by this time. After nearly three and a half years I was let go from my staff job. I told everyone I was going freelance in order to cover my disappointment and embarrassment. After I lost my job I had to pay for my own medical insurance and eventually had to give it up. I couldn't pay for my medication or therapy after that. I had only been able to use the medication for four months.

I was much improved but I needed more help. I had heard from a recovery friend that there was a Twelve Step program for OCD. I went there and felt immediately at home. Since then the OCA meetings and the people there have been of immeasurable help to me in becoming a more serene and productive person.

Recovery, to me, is a process, not a race or contest. Everyone progresses at their own pace. When I first started, going to meetings was enough. Then as I learned more about the steps I saw their value and decided to work them for myself. I found that as I made the effort to follow the program I got significantly better. By the time I had worked all Twelve Steps for the first time I had made a lot of progress. Now I endeavor to work the program every day, even if all I can do on a particular day is just say the Serenity Prayer. As the slogan says, Easy Does It.

The Twelve Step program has been described as a bridge back to life. For me it has been. Today, my productivity is steadily improving and I am rebuilding my reputation as a reliable worker.

During the nearly ten years that I have been in recovery I have made a lot of progress in learning how to live a fuller life. I don't want OCD to waste my time and energy as much as it has. Thank God, it doesn't have to. I may never be totally cured from OCD, but I believe that every day I can get better. With my Higher Power's help and the help of my friends in the fellowship I hope to realize more and more the fuller life I seek. May you find this hope also.

(19)
Not the Twelve-Step Type

I have been plagued most of my life with rituals and obsessions. There seemed to be no logical explanation for these actions, except for the unresolved conflicts and unconscious desires originally offered as explanations by the medical community. I am a medical doctor and it's surprising to me that I was able to go through my schooling plagued by these rituals. It was during this period that I noticed my life seemed to be guided by rituals, while at the same time I did not believe that anything was out of control. In reality my life was very much out of control. I was not able to think clearly. I was not able to understand what people were saying to me and thus I was not able to respond to people when they spoke to me. My personality became imprisoned in the rituals and obsessions.

I guess most things in life are timing and that's the way it was with me. In the late eighties, the psychiatric community finally took notice of many disorders and realized that they might be a result of hyperactivity in the brain and not completely psychological. It was only then that these issues could be properly addressed. My life was becoming increasingly unmanageable and as a result of this I sought serious help. I was diagnosed as having Obsessive Compulsive Disorder for the first time by a leading psychiatrist specializing in this disorder.

While initiating treatment with psychotherapy and medications I was encouraged to seek a form of group therapy. A family member had suggested that I contact a group by the name of Obsessive Compulsive Anonymous. I must add that I had never been in a group discussion since I was in college and I found it very uncomfortable. I had never spoken to a group about my personal problems and I was very self-conscious. At any rate, I contacted OCA with an open mind since I have a medical background, and I made my way to the OCA meeting at a local church.

I can remember my first time. The group consisted of about fifteen people. Each person was discussing what was on their mind and how the group discussions had helped them. I remember being embarrassed for them and being embarrassed for myself. The feeling of shame was almost too hard to bear. As I continued to listen I began to identify more and more with what the people were saying, but my heart was still pounding.

When it was my turn to speak I could barely speak. I still did not feel part of the group. I will tell you this though: the emotional level of the group was high and did not seem to be encumbered by the usual restraints that society puts on itself as a whole. I began to realize while listening to all of the people talking that they had similar conflicts that I had and that many of the conflicts were probably brought about by our common obsessive-compulsive behavior. It was mesmerizing and at the same time refreshing to hear people speak their minds openly in front of me. My rigorous training in my field had kept me from being able to focus in on this type of emotion.

I continued to enjoy the open forum of this group and to attend meetings on a weekly basis. The unconditional acceptance that I received from the group helped me to accept myself for who I was and helped me to reintegrate into society. I continue to look forward to weekly meetings. Thus it is five years later and I have rarely missed a meeting. I must mention the fact that I do not consider myself a typical Twelve Step person, however certain topics that are dealt with in this type of meeting are essential, in my opinion, to one's recovery from the symptoms of OCD. There are certain resentments that we continue to nurture as well as a lack of acceptance of our human condition. By attending meetings such as this we can learn to accept our own human condition and break away from our own internal restrictions. For in reality there is no shame in being a human being. The shame is when we do nothing to modulate our emotions and we go on blindly in life, upsetting ourselves and others.

I continue to participate in OCA meetings and OCA-sponsored activities. The meetings are a source of inspiration and I believe can strengthen the individual, give him insight into himself and the people around him. The OCA meetings, I have discovered, will work if you keep coming back as I have done over the years. I thank the organization for this opportunity to express myself. Have a nice life.

(20)
Gained Control by Letting Go

I remember when this (OCD) first came on in junior high school. I stood by my locker and opened and closed it, checking to make sure everything was in its right place. Everything had to be perfectly straight. I checked it over and over again until I was sure that someone was watching me, and thought I was nuts.

My life was made up of many of these rituals. I took incredibly long showers, scrubbing every part of my body until I was red as a lobster. I later blamed it on the hot water. I did this every time I washed my hands too. It seemed that everything I touched was somehow contaminated.

My nighttime ritual then followed. I checked to make sure everything was turned off. At that point I had also developed special numbers – numbers that were good and numbers that were bad. Each time I checked plugs, light switches, doors and appliances, I did so a certain number of times. Once I reached my designated number (and not accidently gotten a bad number instead), I had to be sure it was safe and not doubt myself. If I had one single doubt (even if I was already in bed), I had to go back and check all over again, which was exhausting!

I remember that contamination and checking were the two symptoms with which the OCD began. I have also had many other symptoms that either disappeared or got better. At times when I am reading, I have a need to reread certain lines a specific number of times. This happens when I am either not concentrating or I'm not sure I am getting all the information (there goes my doubting again!). All this reverts back to my good and bad numbers. When I was attending college and reading for my courses, I could spend hours reading one short chapter and still not be sure I had grasped everything.

It wasn't until several years later that I realized I had OCD. I had heard there was going to be a discussion on the show 20/20 and they were going to interview people who washed their hands over and over again and still felt dirty. That sounded like me! I secretly watched the show, hoping no one would discover me, (as if no one hadn't already noticed I spent hours washing or checking things).

Soon after seeing this show, I found the book, *The Boy Who Couldn't Stop Washing,* and officially recognized myself as having OCD. I was so thrilled to put a name to this insanity; I reentered myself into therapy. This was the beginning of getting help for myself. I contacted the OC Foundation, became a member and found out about the OCA Twelve Step Program. What a relief to meet others who were suffering from the same disorder.

I learned about the steps, but didn't really become involved for about six months. This wasn't because I didn't want to help myself – believe me, I did. I just had problems accepting certain steps. I didn't have a problem accepting Step One; the OCD definitely was more powerful than me, and my life was certainly unmanageable. When addressing Step Two, I mostly believed that a Higher Power could take this away from me, but actually giving up my life and will to a Higher Power really frightened me. I wanted to be in control of my life and what happened to it. Of course, the more I thought about it, the more ridiculous it sounded. There was no way I could be in complete control of my life. I couldn't be completely sure that as I walked across the street I wouldn't get hit by a car or something similar wouldn't happen. As much as I wanted to be sure, and as cautious as I tried to be, there wasn't a one hundred percent guarantee that these things wouldn't happen. Besides, I knew as I went into a checking ritual with the thought, "just one more time," that it really wouldn't be that one last time, for it never was.

I decided I had to give up my control in order to get better... but how? I discussed this with a friend with OCD and he encouraged me to pray. Well, that led to my next problem. I believed in a Higher Power, but I had an OCD issue pertaining to prayer. I ritualized religious readings and prayers. I was afraid that praying would become a ritual, and if I missed it once or didn't pray exactly right, something bad would happen, (magical thinking, I was told). However, I became convinced that this was all due to OCD and to just try it a little. I went home that night and thought, "What do I have to lose? It's worth a try." I didn't completely believe it would work, but I remember hearing once, "Fake it till you believe it."

That's just what I did. I pretended it would work, and much to my surprise, within a few days I noticed a change. It was a miracle. I was able to begin to let go. I wasn't cured, but I was able to say, "Stop, look at what you're doing. You can walk away from this." I now firmly believe that a person must give up control in order to gain control. It may sound crazy, but as I gave up my control and prayed for my Higher Power to help me, it was like my Higher Power gave me control and allowed me to begin to let go. What an awesome feeling it was to not be stuck in a ritual or obsessive thought for hours. I had hit a point of recovery.

Now just as prayers had helped, (and meditations that I began reading on a daily basis), so did other things. I moved out of my parents' house into an apartment, and this helped me a lot. I could step away from problems that were there and see how it all affected me. I could then work on becoming a more functional person.

Another big step in my life was coming to terms with a major issue that had affected me dramatically – being a victim of sexually inappropriate behavior by family members. As my Higher Power's will allowed me, I found support group meetings in the area and began to deal with these issues. As I began to address this, I also noticed that my OCD was reducing even more. However, when I didn't want to deal with these issues and pushed them aside, the opposite happened, and my OCD got worse. Therefore, I was challenged to learn how to deal with both at the same time. This was exhausting but worth it.

I attribute my recovery to so many factors – prayer, meditation, becoming dependent on a Higher Power, dealing with family issues, and most important, becoming part of the Twelve Step Program that includes the steps, the group, and the support I receive. In no way am I cured of my OCD. In fact, during periods of stress, I have "OCD setbacks." I find that anger and emotional instability antagonize my OCD, but I'm learning how to handle setbacks better each time. I know that I don't have to do it alone!

I am very grateful for this program. I incorporate it into all parts of my life and feel healthier as a result of that. I now try to use all that I have learned, including the slogan, "One day at a time," to deal with my OCD. I am so grateful to everything that has helped me to lead a more functional life. I now hope I can reach out to others and help them as I've been helped through this program of recovery.

(21)
Progressive Recovery

I'm thirty-three years old and have OCD. Many people have asked me, "When did your OCD start?" I don't believe anyone can really answer that question because OCD comes in so many shapes and sizes. I can remember always doing compulsive actions. I remember my need to touch the top step of the staircase twice, to make sure that my right shoe was always farther forward on the floor than my left shoe and that the dollar bills in my wallet faced the same way. Also I wasn't able to move at a traffic signal until I looked at the green light four times. I could go on and on describing all the different compulsions I've had throughout my life. If I didn't perform them I usually believed it meant something bad would happen, so I just did them (which seemed so stupid to me and was always so time consuming).

Two years ago, after having been married for two years, I separated from my husband. My son was nine months old and we moved back home with my parents because I had nowhere else to go. I started attending Divorce Separation Anonymous (DSA) groups and after about two months I started to feel like my old self again. I had many close friends, but most were married. When the weekends rolled around I felt so alone. Through DSA though, I began to find new, single friends – people with whom I could do things. Most important, these people were *so* supportive; after all, they were in my shoes too. That's the terrific thing about support groups – everyone knows exactly what the other members are talking about and often, even what they're feeling.

Approximately six months later I started thinking "bad thoughts" about my fifteen-month old son. It seemed so odd that I would be having such violent and aggressive thoughts about someone I loved. As the thoughts became more frequent my body began shaking from anxiety and fear. I had insomnia for three nights and I believe that these thoughts dominated me because I was so tired.

Since my psychiatrist was on vacation at the time, I saw his colleague who told me I was having "delayed post-partum depression," which could occur up to three years after birth. He suggested that I stay in the hospital for a while to rest. This rest period led to a five-week stay in the hospital. Even though we tried many different medications I was still having horrifying thoughts. Finally I underwent electro-convulsive therapy and it was working well. When I left the hospital my psychiatrist told me he strongly believed that the OCD was what caused my severe depression.

In about two months the thoughts returned with a vengeance and began to torture me once more. I had been dating a wonderful fellow for a month who saw the intensity of the pain I was in. Together we searched for a support group for people with OCD since my psychiatrist had told me it is very common.

After spending an entire morning on the telephone trying to find an appropriate group, I knew I had found gold when I heard a recorded voice on the other end telling me about OCA. I couldn't wait to buy the book *Obsessive Compulsive Anonymous* at the first meeting I attended. I remember sitting in that meeting crying, shaking and telling the group about my bizarre thoughts. Even though I believed any other group of people would have truly thought I was insane, these people told me I had come to the right place. They also told me that OCD is very common and I knew then and there that these understanding people were going to be my very close friends.

After attending several meetings I started to meet some of

the people whose stories appear in the OCA book. I couldn't believe that these recovering people were the same ones about whose pain and suffering I had read. To me, this was the definition of recovery.

I was desperate at the time and I remember thinking, "If they can do it, I can do it." I had to remind myself that my goal was to get better. I knew the process would be slow, requiring patience and persistence in working my program, everyone I knew in recovery told me, "I don't know how it works, but it works." Some of the suggestions made by other members of the program to help in my recovery included:

Attend Twelve Step workshops to help me work the steps.
Perform service in OCA, participate in the fellowship
    and at meetings.
Use the telephone list that usually circulated through the
    meeting by calling other program people to share our
    experiences, which helps them as much as it helps me.
Practice the principles of the Twelve Steps and read
    Twelve Step literature daily.

I've come a long way in eight months. My progress has been slow, but as it is said in all Twelve Step programs, "We didn't get this way overnight, so we can't expect to get better overnight." I still have bizarre thoughts, but they're not as bad as they once were, which shows me that I'm on the road to recovery – where I'm supposed to be. I've also learned by reading various OCD-related books, from the OCA program and my psychiatrist that my "brand" of OCD is the most common.

I've found that most of the members of OCA are highly intelligent individuals who are living in reality and, therefore, don't act on their thoughts, knowing that they are just thoughts. Everyone in the world has a bizarre thought now and then, but people with OCD aren't able to stop thinking their thoughts (it's a vicious cycle). The best thing about OCA is that regardless of our individual obsessions or compulsions, no one is alone in this program. The program works if you work it!

(22)
My Journey Back to Me

I am a recovering addict. My recovery includes recovering from OCD, which I have come to accept as a "process" addiction, as opposed to a chemical addiction. In writing my story for OCA, I am choosing to name all of my addictions because my recovery has taught me that my OCD does not operate in a vacuum; it is significantly influenced by my other addictive processes. Unfortunately though, it also has a life of its own.

My earliest recollection of my OCD was during the summer between kindergarten and first grade. I kept getting the name of my first grade teacher mixed up with the name of the US President at that time. All summer long I asked my mother what my teacher's name was. My mother reassured me that it was not the President and my fear would go away (until the next time).

I do not recall being very "present" in high school. I was an honor student, studied hard when I felt like it and cheated on exams when I did not study. I have vivid memories of daydreaming in class and worrying about my dog. I had an almost constant low-level obsession about his safety (would he run out the door when my dad came home? Was he all right?) and so on. During my first two years of high school I spent virtually all my free time by myself. I had no friends. During junior year my dad let me use the family car and I quickly became popular since I was one of the first guys in school to have a car.

I had friends all around me from then on. I was leading a double life; maintaining high grades in school while hanging out with my friends and acting out with sex and prescription drugs. I developed serious crushes (in reality, severe obsessions) on a variety of people, which in recovery I have come to realize were the genesis of my romance and relationship addiction.

My home life was nothing to brag about back then. My father's alcoholism was progressing, my sister was abusing uppers (for diet reasons of course), I had my own prescription to "help me get to sleep" and my mother was trying her best to control the family. I always wanted to escape the constant pain.

In college my addictions progressed. I was so unwilling to sleep alone that if I had to, I took tranquilizers obtained via a stolen prescription pad. I isolated severely, carried a full course load, worked nearly forty hours a week at a local hospital and played the organ at a church on weekends (back then I did not know the meaning of workaholism — all I knew was my dad was an alcoholic and come hell or high water, I was not going to turn out like him).

OCD made its adult onset during graduate school, in my mid-twenties. At that time I was working at least fifty hours a week (and obsessing about work when I was not in the office), going to class, playing the organ and studying during the weekend. Who needed friends? I was just too "busy" all the time. I remember working until nine on a Friday night and going home to clean my apartment. I was addicted to my own adrenaline – I got hits from being busy and rushing. (Today my busyaholism and rushaholism can trigger my OCD.)

One night, while sitting in class, the panic hit. "What was the name of _____?" I could not remember. The panic grew worse. Hard as I tried, I could not remember. Of course I went home and took another pill to relieve the anxiety until I eventually remembered the name. More often than not, the obsession was replaced with another one and another panic attack about something else I just could *not* remember.

So it went on progressively for years and years. At my bottom I added compulsive cruising for sex, late night workouts (addicted to exercise? Not me of course), eating a half quart of ice cream before bed and "dealing with" the OCD by taking more and more tranquilizers.

That downward spiral continued until April, 1989, when I walked into my first SLAA (Sex and Love Addicts Anonymous) meeting. I kept going to meetings, but my disease kept progressing because I was traveling around the country as a consultant and I did not avail myself of the supportive fellowship of other people in recovery.

I made lists of things I might "forget" in the future. I thought I could lick this craziness that was going on in my head. I fantasized about having a large data base where I could keep making entries about things I was afraid I would forget. Yes, that would be the answer to all my problems: Then if the panic hit, all I would have to do was look it up on the computer. My disease was – and is – very cunning.

A typical day for me back then ended with trying to fall asleep in my hotel room, only to have more "missing information" panic attacks. I made frantic telephone calls back home – sometimes to people I had not talked to in years to find out someone's dog's name or the name of a hot dog stand in our old neighborhood. The shame and embarrassment of this was unbearable. The turning point came when I called a friend in South America for the answer to a trivial question.

At that time I was being treated for OCD with tranquilizers and antidepressants, but experiencing bad side effects. My gut told me I was wasting my time with practitioners who knew nothing about addictions. When I stopped taking prescription drugs, I experienced an excruciating withdrawal. By January, 1991, I was in a treatment center for Post Traumatic Stress Disorder, as well as for addiction treatment. For the first time in my life I was feeling my feelings and dealing with them. Paradoxically my OCD almost disappeared during treatment.

I continued to work my recovery program and to gain clarity about my addictions. I had reached such a level of devastation that I needed an extended period of time away from work in order to get my life back together. I applied for long-term Disability benefits.

So many things were lifted through my Higher Power. My craving for drugs was greatly reduced. As of this writing, I have not used a mood-altering chemical for over two years. My craving for anonymous sex was lifted. I began to address my workaholism, relationship addiction, and incest issues. Throughout all of this, OCD continued to take place in my life with waxing and waning symptoms. Yet one thing became clear; the more willing I was to face my feelings and actually *feel* them (I'm not talking about writing them down or experiencing them in my head) the less room OCD had in my life.

I was working steps Six and Seven for the removal of OCD (I thought it was just a character defect), when my counselor lent me OCA's book. I was both happy and angry – happy that there was a fellowship and angry that I had to work yet another program. For years my counselor had told me that the OCD sounded like just another form of the addictive process and I would need to work the steps on it. I was adamant: No way would I work the steps on something as powerful as OCD – those crazy thunderstorms that kept going off in my head.

Within weeks of reading OCA's book, I was in New York City attending my first OCA meeting. I felt love and acceptance as well as gratitude toward the thirty people who were at the meeting. The topic of that meeting was "taking risks," and I spoke about my risk-taking and willingness to go to any lengths to recover from OCD. Shortly thereafter I returned home, and Chicago's first OCA meeting was held.

My OCD still wants to hold on for dear life and I have to

acknowledge that, as with any addiction, it is progressive and fatal. Several years ago I attempted suicide during one attack.

OCA was not the panacea I thought it would be. I am, however, experiencing a slow system shift and am becoming more accepting of my powerlessness over this disease. What I know about my recovery process is that my life became more manageable as I began to accept my powerlessness over my various addictions. Acceptance did not happen overnight. My recovery has taught me that recovery is more than just reciting the steps – it's about living the steps.

Today I still have OCD attacks, but they are not as frequent as in my pre-recovery days. The Twelve Step program works in treating compulsive diseases and I know in my heart that it works for OCD as well. Today I am looking forward to returning to a job that is sober for me. I've begun writing a book of poetry and I feel my creativity just begging to be let out of the prison where it was held captive for so many years.

I believe all of us who have OCD are very special. I also believe that our specialness and creativity was held in check by our disease and the Twelve Step program is our way back to ourselves. I struggle with my program frequently. The, slogan "progress, not perfection" is very important to me. I'm finally learning to live life on its own terms, not mine, and that can be painful. Despite these ups and downs, I'd like to close my story with what I now say at the close of every meeting I attend, "Keep coming back-it's *working!*"

(23)
A Martyr's Story

I'm thirty-eight years old and I've had OCD almost all my life. I can trace the onset of my illness to when I was about five years old. I am a "thinker." I was always trying to understand and figure out the things I encountered. When I was as young as four I dwelled on things my parents told me.

Since my brothers and sisters were at school during the day, I spent most of my time alone except when I went shopping with my mother. My mother was always busy doing housework and didn't spend much time reading to me or doing fun things with me. She never hugged us and was always dramatic and serious. She referred to people as the "haves" and the "have-nots," focusing mostly on the negative aspects of things and on people who suffered a lot. I felt very guilty for having so much (although I now realize I actually had very little) when other children had much less.

My father, to whom I felt the closest, was a hero to me. He wasn't very handy, which contributed to my low self-esteem. He was, however, very sensitive to other people's feelings, so I was taught to think of other people first and not to be "selfish." I took this to the extreme and felt I could never have anything for myself. I denied myself things because I was afraid they would be taken from me. I didn't realize how much OCD had distorted my thinking.

Most of my problems revolved around "scrupulosity." I always questioned whether things were right or wrong. I felt I was an evil person. I couldn't accept my thoughts and feelings as normal and therefore also believed I was sinning. I truly believed I should always be perfect.

I was raised as a Catholic and attended parochial school. When I was about six years old I obsessed about what I should tell the priest during confession. I felt something was wrong if I didn't find some sin to confess. I thought I was committing a mortal sin and violating one of the Ten Commandments because I was attracted to a married woman who lived on the block. I thought I was sinning when I had my own sexual feelings.

I also constantly asked God how God could let some people suffer more than others. I was very affected by a son of my mother's friend who was paralyzed from the waist down. On a vacation, when I was eight years old, my father suffered a heart attack after he insisted on carrying this boy. I felt people had to be martyrs and this was the way life was supposed to be. After spending six months in bed my father decided to go back to work regardless of the doctor's warnings that he not go. During the first week back he suffered another heart attack and died. I cried and felt I was the only one who showed any feelings. When my mother said, "You just have to go on," I thought that meant she didn't love my father (not-true). At my father's wake I felt as though I was "sick" because I allowed people to make me laugh and I enjoyed having dinner in a restaurant, as well as all the excitement and attention. I kept asking myself how I could be happy and how I could lack feelings when my father had just died.

All of these events triggered my OCD symptoms. After my father died I spent a lot of time questioning the existence of God. I repeated my prayers because I felt I wasn't saying them right. I was afraid I would go to hell for not behaving as my religion dictated. I jumped over cracks in the sidewalk, believing if I could cross the line before a car passed me, I would go to heaven.

I also had trouble knowing how to act with friends. I felt I didn't belong and somehow people would think I was a "goody-goody." I couldn't carry on a conversation, so I acted silly. I also wanted a girlfriend very much, but my OCD wasn't going to let me have one. It threw everything in my path to prevent me from getting what I wanted.

At that time I suffered from depression, which was to recur throughout my life. When my mother and brother were fighting, I had thoughts about murdering my mother. I realized I was losing sight of reality and no longer had any feelings – good or bad. I was so scared I was going to murder her that I sat for hours trying to think things through and praying for God's help.

I developed unpleasant sensations in my mouth and face, which later became an uncomfortable tightness in my neck and shoulders (somatization), which I still have. I began feeling paranoia; I believed people were looking at me and even laughing at me. I also had sexual thoughts about women and felt sinful about that. To counteract these thoughts I tried thinking about men instead. However, my OCD told me that maybe I desired men too – that was too much for me to handle. I later learned that these types of thoughts are very normal.

I was so alone, withdrawn and hurting emotionally. My murderous thoughts turned against anyone – I had desires to push people in front of trains or stab them. I feared I would do these things. I even wanted to sexually harm my brother's children. After mentioning these thoughts at an OCA meeting, I learned other people had them too – much to my surprise. OCD has no limits! I took a big risk by disclosing this at the meeting, but trusting paid off – I found out I was not alone. As my sponsor told me, "We are as sick as our secrets."

When I went to college in 1972, I had no interests in life, no hobbies and I couldn't make decisions for myself. After trying to succeed in college for two and a half years, my OCD became overwhelming. Having little interest in the courses I had chosen, I decided to leave the school. I acknowledged I was the one who had to do something about this illness, I had to tell someone and take action. I spoke with a priest in my parish and began seeing a psychotherapist.

After several psychotherapy sessions, I believed I was getting the proper treatment for my illness because some of my murderous thoughts were subsiding. I couldn't understand, though, why a lot of checking rituals were taking over my life. I took an hour and a half to get to bed because I checked everything on my desk over and over to ensure each item was in order, but I was never satisfied. I had to force myself to stop! I was afraid that if I didn't check, someone would get hurt or a fire would start. My showers lasted for more than two hours and it took me twenty minutes to get out of the car. I also checked my pants pockets more than thirty times to make sure I didn't leave anything in them.

Eventually my sister showed me an article about OCD and a medicine that was being tested for the disorder. I realized that I had OCD, not a simple neurosis as my therapist had said. I eventually telephoned an OCD organization and got into a medication research study. I became more sociable and after three months was directed to behavior modification therapy. This therapy alleviated most of my checking rituals. I started socializing again after five years of isolation. I went to dances and started to make new friends and meet women. However, I began obsessing about hurting women's feelings, finding the perfect woman and how to end dates. I drifted in and out of depression for many years because I wasn't getting into a relationship.

Through a newsletter from one of the dances I learned about an OCD self-help group. At the very first OCA meeting I knew for the first time in my life where I belonged. I was ready for a different way and was attracted to the Twelve Steps because of its humanistic and spiritual approach. After hearing other people's stories about how their lives had changed and how much help they received from the program, I wanted to have what they had. I thank God to this day that I had the willingness to do all I could do to get better. At that first OCA meeting I asked how I could get a sponsor.

The program allowed me to realize what I was doing wrong: I was always telling God what I wanted God to do for me instead of asking, "What does God want me to do?" With the help of a priest who is familiar with OCD, I learned that a person could pray "too much." My mind was so rigid that I couldn't imagine God wanting a person to "lighten up." Once I gave my will over to God in Step Three, and stopped telling God what I wanted done for me, my life started to change. I now feel God wants a lot of the things I want for myself and will help me to get them faster if I let go.

Giving service really helped to advance my recovery. I was afraid to take a suggestion to become the meeting's treasurer – my OCD told me I was going to steal the money. The OCD always tried to prevent me from doing things. To my amazement, within a few months I also began leading meetings. The idea of this had seemed almost impossible to me; my OCD had created endless reasons why I shouldn't lead meetings. Eventually I told myself, "So what (if I make a mistake or say something wrong). I'm growing, taking risks and getting better." In spite of what my OCD tells me, I find that "hanging in there" pays off. I didn't realize recovery would be such a struggle – although well worth it!

After serving my term as chairman and through OCA telephone calls I began to change. I grew out of my isolation and began showing concern for others. I became outgoing and was able to have conversations with people, including women – my fears of hurting their feelings had subsided. I learned that

I'm not so weird; other people have similar thoughts. I really do find that the more I give, the more I get. There is nothing more rewarding than having someone in the program tell me how much I've helped them.

When I did my Fourth and Fifth steps with my sponsor, I felt some resentments lift and realized that my thinking had become clearer. I could actually learn and grow from my experiences. I needed to clean up my side of the street in order to let God's grace into my life. I really feel God is guiding me; I pray for freedom from self-will and to be able to let go. Now when I am going through a rough time I ask, "What are you trying to show me?" The path of recovery is not easy and sometimes I just want to give up, but I know the alternative is pain and no growth. The program is the antidote to my OCD.

I now try to challenge the lies I tell myself and can quickly change negative OCD thoughts into positive recovery thoughts before they can pull me down. I challenge the irrational beliefs with rational ones. All I had to do was *want* to get better. Willingness is very difficult for many people, but if we pray for it we will be shown the way.

I know some people don't believe in a God and therefore think they can't work the program. This is not true. A person's Higher Power can be anything that person wants it to be – the group, nature or anything that works for that person. Not believing in a God doesn't have to hold anyone back from reaping the benefits of this program. I know people who have "acted as if" they believed in a God and have gotten better.

Before entering this program I remember having joy only a few times in my life. I now have comfort in knowing I have friends who understand and support me. I was very wrong in thinking I could solve my problems by myself. I thought my judgment was perfect, but this was probably due to my OCD.

I am so thankful to God and to my friends in OCA for helping me find the Twelve Steps as a way to recover from OCD. I know I have a long way to go and may always have OCD, but through the program I'll have more of life and will always be growing and getting better.

(24)
Out of My Head and Into My Heart

My OCD began almost as far back as my memory goes-my rituals started off being only at night – I would cry myself to sleep at times because I couldn't stop the obsessions and compulsions, and I had no idea what was wrong with me; I just assumed this was my "job."

I believe I grew up with a lot of shame and lowered self-esteem due to this disease. I don't know if something happened to "set off" my OCD – but today, it doesn't really matter – what matters is that I get out of my head and into my feelings, my soul! I've realized I am powerless to negotiate with this disease. Oh sure, it will trick me into thinking if I analyze it and give in to my thinking compulsions, the pain will stop. It turns out to be a quick fix that only serves to add fuel to the fire of the disease.

As I write this I am on my first day of vacation in Arizona – today was really hard with the OCD – I miss the connection and help I receive from making outreach calls to my program friends. People from my Twelve Step programs have been able to help me in ways no one else ever has! Maybe this is just God's way of bringing us together,

Today when I'm struggling with my disease, I pray, read, write, or make a call. Usually this helps tremendously – when it doesn't, I pray for acceptance, help to focus on something besides my OCD, and try to remind myself that "This too shall pass." I'm defiant – I like to be comfortable and OCD is anything but comfortable!

Today I also take medication – something that has helped me a lot – I don't plan to take it forever; my goal is to become healthier mentally, emotionally and physically, and to become better able to deal effectively and sanely with relationships and issues in my life – thereby not being "triggered" as easily into OCD. I believe, for me, OCD is "triggered" by feelings I don't want or know (how to feel). It's not my fault; it just is.

Today, usually when I'm feeling depressed or lonely, it's because I've lost connection with myself and my Higher Power. It's a habit for me to live in my head instead of in my heart. My head tells me I'll be safe there, but the truth is, it's a prison with no escape. Living in my heart, my feelings seem scarier, but it's the way to freedom, joy and life!

God Bless all of you.

(25)
Choose Faith

I started to pick at my skin when I was about ten years old because I thought my skin was ugly - freckly and bumpy. Any little bump or blemish that appeared on my body had to be removed. I also believed these bumps were pimples because my skin was dirty. After visits to several dermatologists, I learned that the dry skin bumps, mostly on my arms and legs, had become impetigo, which spreads terribly if broken open. Most of the time I would pick my skin until it bled. Then I sterilized the area with rubbing alcohol and antibacterial creams. Thus my compulsion of picking and cleaning was born.

I am also an alcoholic and I came into Alcoholics Anonymous when I was twenty-two years old. My life improved dramatically when I got sober and adopted the Twelve Step program as a road map for living. Having just graduated from college, I got a job and was living on my own, struggling with accepting such a radically new way of life. Although I was beginning to like myself a little bit, my picking compulsion became worse. I increasingly isolated myself to spend more and more time picking.

I loved the beautiful summers in Chicago, but I could never wear shorts or sleeveless shirts because my skin was covered with scabs. I was planning to take a vacation with new A.A. friends and because I knew I would be wearing a bathing suit around men, I controlled the compulsion for a week prior to the trip. That experience turned out to be the start of another wonderful change in my life. One of my new friends was the man I later married.

I moved to Orlando, Florida. I then found I had more time to isolate and perform my compulsions. I loved the bright, sunny windows in my house where I could spend hours and hours finding all the imperfections on my skin. But throughout the hot Florida summers I wore long pants and shirts, terrified I would ever be asked to go to the beach or anywhere I might be expected to wear shorts.

One month after we were married, my husband went away to codependency treatment. I went the next month. The individual and couples therapy I received over the next four years saved my marriage.

My husband became increasingly angry when I spent countless hours in the bathroom in front of the mirror or hunched over my arms and legs. If I was under stress or felt out of control, usually because of school or my marriage, the compulsions became worse. I was so ashamed of my strange habits that I did not want to tell anyone; I tried to stop on my own.

I bought every imaginable pimple cream, soap and lotion. I burned my skin in the sun. I went to a hypnotist. I started to look through medical and psychological books because I knew what I was doing to myself was not normal. I was so sick and could not stop. How could the God that brought me to A.A. and counseling allow me to continue to destroy myself?

Then one day at the library, I saw *The Boy Who Couldn't Stop Washing.* Drawn to this book, I read about the ritualistic behaviors and compulsions and I saw myself. Obsessive-Compulsive Disorder. Finally! A name I could put to this insanity that ruled my life. I called some of the telephone numbers in the book and was eventually given the number of a woman who had started an OCA meeting in Florida.

I did not call right away, but when I did she told me about a program of Twelve Steps modeled after A.A. that was for people suffering with OCD. She told me that she had found recovery through this program. I cried when I hung up the phone. I was powerless over OCD and my life was definitely unmanageable.

I went to my first meeting and listened as they shared their experiences with this disease, their strength with the program and their hope for other sufferers. Although the details of their stories were different from mine, I identified with the feelings – fear, hopelessness, isolation and shame. While I was not sure that the program could work for me, I believed that it was working for the other people and this was my ray of hope. I came to believe that God could restore me to sanity.

My husband and I moved overseas where there were no meetings. I read the OCA book and I corresponded with my sponsor and other recovering OCAs but my biggest struggle was the subject of abstinence. Because I had to be one hundred percent abstinent with alcohol, I thought I had to be one hundred percent abstinent with my OCD rituals. They told me that in OCA our goal is not total abstinence – but *recovery*.

My sponsor said that as she worked the steps, she shifted her focus on to living and the rituals lost their importance. She said she had to put God first and trust Him in *everything*. I have found this Third Step to work in my life too: "We made a decision to turn our will and our lives over to the care of God as we understood Him."

The peace of mind and joy for life that I have experienced in the OCA program is something that I believed was never possible for me. I thank Father Leo Booth and all the members of OCA who have helped me to start to understand that I am that miracle.

(26)
Faith into Action

I'm recovering from OCD. The foundation of my recovery is my Higher Power, Jesus Christ, at work in OCA. OCA helped me to put my faith into action.

I've been suffering from OCD since I was a kid. I have been through all of the major OCD symptoms. Early in my life I had washing compulsions. They faded away in time, but were replaced by checking rituals. I was always late due to these rituals. I've always been fighting my rituals, but not always successfully. Often when I thought I had overcome certain rituals they were immediately replaced by other ones. Unaided willpower is incapable of overcoming OCD.

When I wasn't troubled by OCD I had other psychological troubles such as anxiety and an inferiority complex (e.g., my nose had an ugly shape or our family was foreign and partly Jewish in a homogenous Swedish society). I felt insecure dealing with people, afraid of just not being good enough.

In my teens I had a break from OCD. However, I had problems in school. My teachers regarded me as a pest, destroying their classes by talking and not paying attention. For a two-week period I was sent to an observation class, which was my turning point in school. The teachers threatened if I didn't change and pull myself together, I was going to remain in the observation class through junior high school. I did change and improved my grades in only a few months.

After graduating from high school I pursued a college degree. I attended classes for five years, studying full time. Despite this, I hardly took any of the exams on time. I always had to take make-up exams. By failing in my studies I no longer qualified for Government Student Loans. Then I supported myself on inherited money. Later I received unemployment benefits and Social Welfare. During my years as a student I had only a few summer jobs. What did I do during all those years? I did have a longlasting, dynamic, gay relationship. But I spent most of the time by myself obsessing, performing compulsions and ruminating like a madman. My OCD thoughts made it impossible to fully concentrate on my studies. The OCD made me into an introvert.

I repeatedly ruminated about my voice being too high pitched. I knew from the beginning that I had a normally pitched voice for a man. However, I was completely unable to let go of that meaningless thought. This was the powerful force of doubt. How could I really know my voice was okay? I recorded myself on a cassette. It gave me satisfaction for a day. The next day I questioned how I could really know that the playback was accurate.

I asked my lover, "How does my voice sound?"

He said, "Normal."

"How does my voice sound?" I asked again.

"For the last time, normal."

When I sensed him getting annoyed, I would vary the question: "Do I have a high-pitched voice?"

I still wasn't satisfied, but I knew asking more questions would not help. I didn't know what to do, nor did my lover. In the long run the doubt always came back, stronger and louder than ever before.

Finally, years after the "voice" thought first emerged, I went to see a speech therapist. He told me I had a normally pitched voice. Of course, what he said didn't satisfy me. The terrifying loop of OCD thinking got more control over my mind the more I tried to get rid of it.

Due to a miracle I got a scholarship to the US as an exchange student. A few years before, I had been in psychodynamic therapy. The therapist was also gay, which made it easier for me to trust him. The therapy helped me to reflect on my emotions and my life. I saw going to the States as a possibility to change my life. I felt very motivated to do well.

This strong motivation enabled me to concentrate on my school work during those years in Los Angeles. However, other areas of my life were affected by OCD. Since it took me so long to study, there was no time to socialize. After two years proving to myself that I could study if I only tried hard enough, I relapsed once again into overt OCD behavior. I wasn't able to do anything besides worrying and checking.

Back in Switzerland I got depressed and spent a weekend at an emergency clinic for suicidal patients. I had the feeling my life was going nowhere due to my OCD. During my young adulthood I received a lot of psychiatric diagnoses: neurotic with isolation and intellectualizing as psychological defense mechanisms; psychotic, borderline case; and manic depressive. Now for the first time I got a diagnosis I felt was accurate and the MD suggested medication. Since I was going to commit suicide, I had nothing to lose. However, I had to discontinue taking medication due to unbearable side-effects.

I've always been a Christian. A year ago my faith took on another dimension. I had a spiritual awakening shortly before joining OCA. Nothing happened externally, it was something inside of me that had always been there. It took a leap into my consciousness. I realized the power of God. Working through the Twelve Steps led to another spiritual awakening. My spirituality gets deeper every day. It brings me closer to God. In OCA I met people who were doing something for themselves. OCA made it possible for me to put my faith into action.

Since returning to Sweden, I've been trying to organize an

OCA group. So far I've been moderately successful. I've encountered skepticism about the Twelve Step tradition, especially from professionals. Some psychiatrists, however, have encouraged me to persevere with starting an OCA group. I also find it helpful to go to other Twelve Step groups when they have open meetings. Our problems might differ, but the way we try to get better is the same.

It's not strange that some people with OCD shrink away from OCA. OCA asks us to do exactly what is most difficult to do: accept ourselves and be honest, let go of resentments, stop thinking only about ourselves and leave our lives in the care of a Higher Power. I think there is a connection between dishonesty, being full of resentment and feeling external pressure and OCD. OCD can make us self-centered by putting our focus on our fears and on being too careful most of the time. OCA requires a change of attitude. I think that is why many of us have to hit bottom before we can stay in OCA.

Besides Christ and OCA, some simple behavior and cognitive techniques are responsible for my recovery. The most important component of these techniques is acceptance. Accept what you are afraid of. All people with OCD have insight. They don't really think they *have* to do what they feel they must be doing or thinking. If you are afraid of germs, accept this fear. Accept there are dangerous germs in the world. In order to prevent myself from washing my hands, I usually think as follows:

It's not likely that there are dangerous germs on my hands. Therefore, I'll not wash my hands, which will increase my anxiety level drastically. But I choose to live with a high level of anxiety because I know the anxiety will decrease in time. And I also know that to keep on washing my hands is not an alternative; it's a dead-end road.

I want to do other things in my life, rather than washing my hands over and over again. I accept the possibility of germs and take a chance on life by asking myself, "What's the worst thing that could happen by not washing? I could die! But if I did – so what? I don't have an alternative. The bottom line has to be: So what?"

Having OCD is not great, but it's not necessarily bad. People with OCD seem to have higher standards. When they do something, they do it properly. They are dependable. When they say they'll call back, they do. OCD might also help in developing a more creative personality. Due to the problems we experience, we are forced to look at life in a different light. The creativity can take us on roads we otherwise might not have taken.

The never-ending process of development is fascinating. We will never be ready. Our characters are only getting more refined through the process we call life.

(27)
Coming Out with OCD

Writing this story is very difficult for me because just the act of writing antagonizes my OCD symptoms. In fact the other night in preparation for this I experienced a panic attack and became overwhelmed with fear. What if I'm not remembering things correctly? Will anyone get in trouble or harmed as a result of my daring to confront my fears?

As long as I can remember I have felt different from most people around me. I was the only left-handed, nonathletic, tone-deaf person in a family of right-handed, athletic, talented musicians. I always felt I didn't quite measure up and as a result, felt judged and criticized. I experienced lots of guilt for being all wrong, as if I was a mistake.

Growing up and discovering I was gay distanced me more because I felt I could not live up in any way to my parents' high expectations. Gaining acceptance and approval was always important, though it seemed an impossible task. It appeared to me that my parents were chronically dissatisfied, which I suspected somehow set off my OCD.

The most debilitating symptoms were:

Responsibility. I felt harm would come to others close to me if I allowed certain feelings to exist such as anger or even good feelings. Although I must have been as young as six or seven when this started, somehow I thought harm could be warded off and controlled by tapping or touching things, or lining up every pencil in the house.

Nervous ticks of my face and eyes. Having to blink a number of times or shake my head without reason was very embarrassing at public school or while playing.

Repetition. I had to read traffic signs and posters to myself repeatedly until it felt right and I could move on. These "thought attacks" also prevented me from shutting off a radio or television unless the correct words were broadcast, or it felt right. If I was alone in the house I had to pull out the plugs from the outlets. There were times when I feared leaving my apartment, thinking the oven would somehow kill my pets or other people in the building.

Religious distortion, or scrupulosity. I had a good deal of difficulty separating OCD and superstitions from religion. In my very early years my grandmother lived with us. Her beliefs seemed pure and spiritual. She had love and respect for G-D and sought comfort in prayer, but also expressed concern, indulgence and protection for us kids. On the other hand, my mother's beliefs seemed based more on fear and punishment than mercy or tolerance. When I was about five and my grandmother moved out, it seemed that my OCD and my mother's rigidity flourished. I reacted to everything with impending doom; superstition, not G-D, became my Higher Power and I no longer felt safe. My childhood memories are all clouded with anxieties, nervousness and attempts on my part to feel safe and protected.

My father was a salesman and often traveled out of town. At these times my mother's fears and her own (apparent) OCD got worse, along with her irrational demands and hysteria. The worse this became, the more I eased G-D out of my life and became arrogant in thinking that I could control the uncontrollable with my rituals and magical thinking, and thus feel safe for the moment. When this seemed to work, it just got more complicated and took up more and more time. The more I submitted to the rules the worse I became. I lost much time fighting to feel in control. The ongoing internal battle was exhausting.

As a result of this constant anxiety and trepidation I began to rely on tranquilizers and overeating to get through the day. After graduating from school and beginning to socialize, I added diet pills, marijuana and, periodically, alcohol to anesthetize myself against what I perceived was a hostile world.

My first Twelve Step program was Overeaters Anonymous (OA). I'm very grateful to OA and A.A. for teaching me how to get by a day at a time without being enabled by substances. I'm grateful to Adult Children of Alcoholics (ACOA) for teaching me the boundaries between myself and other people, and what I'm responsible for and what I'm not. However, I felt as if I was holding back and not able to surrender to these programs enough to be comfortable. Although I led meetings and was sober and abstinent, I felt hypocritical. I wanted the serenity and peace of mind people at meetings spoke about. I still felt that G-D was there for everybody but me. I was being punished because my secret rituals and magical thinking were greater than G-D. This discontent and depression led me to see an addiction counselor.

Recovery began as a result of my perceptive therapist's catching me in one of my rituals. While waiting for him to return to his office, I had noticed the complete set of Freud's books were numerically out of order on a bookshelf, and felt compelled to straighten them out, along with a bump in the carpet. This began a new journey where I was finally correctly diagnosed with OCD and not my greatest fear – insanity.

As a result of the OCA program, behavior therapy and medication, today I can honestly say I have a peace of mind and sense of well being that is totally new. The shame, guilt and other stigmas are hardly there. I can now experience spontaneity and feelings such as anger and joy (which were not permitted in my past world). They feel safe and acceptable, as are all my feelings; there is nothing to hide from. I'm very grateful to know I'm good enough just the way I am.

I don't know what tomorrow will bring, but when I try to live a day at a time and follow the program's suggestions, I feel as if I'm becoming a new person, one who finally does not feel trapped each day without choices, but can live and work from a place of joy and love, not fear.

(28)
One Foot in Front of the Other

I was born in Los Angeles and have lived here all my life. My parents are loving, tolerant, all-around good people. I was raised in an almost totally permissive environment. The only restrictions that were placed on me were based on my parents' fierce desire to protect me.

I believe I was born bodily and mentally different from my fellows. From my first drink at the age of fourteen I drank alcoholically. By my late teens I had become a full-blown alcoholic and drug addict. I had also developed eating disorders, Obsessive-Compulsive disorder and a fairly strong case of Tourette's syndrome. Of course I didn't know then what I had. I sought help at a county mental health facility. The psychiatrist there refused to tell me his diagnosis, but he did point out my drinking problem. He suggested I go to A.A. meetings, but I had been there a few years earlier for a drunk driving offense and I had convinced myself that it was a cult. I told the doctor that much and that's all that was said.

Despite all of the misery I was going through, and even though I desperately wanted to get better, when I tried to stop by myself I lasted a week without a drink and was off again. After that last encounter I never went back to see that doctor again.

This occurred about four and a half years ago. I was hitting bottom with everything at once. I had gone from the anorectic weight of one hundred-twenty pounds (I'm about six feet tall) to one hundred-ninety pounds within a few months of overeating. I was a daily drunk, very often finding myself waking up after an evening blackout feeling utterly ashamed, terrified and baffled by my condition. Also a daily drug user for many years, I smoked marijuana for reasons I could not explain at the time, even though the extreme paranoia it always caused me accentuated my OCD and Tourette's syndrome.

Briefly about my OCD – I am a ruminator – my fears lie in my thoughts. I believe it started when I was in fourth grade when my teacher was talking to me and I was looking up into her eyes. Suddenly I thought, "What if she can read my mind?" So, almost to prove to myself that it was impossible, I *made* myself think horrible, negative thoughts about her. Then the fear grew as the doubt came and I thought, "Can she hear it?"

This fear and process happened from time to time over the years whenever I felt too "close" to someone, but it really wasn't a big deal until I was around seventeen. Caught up in my other fears at that time, I had no defense against taking on new, odd ones – very odd ones. I also believed nobody else could have these fears and so many of them!

Most of the fears were based on the notion of causing harm to others. If I had a "bad thought" such as, "This will kill my mother," I had to reverse it toward myself: "*I* will die." I had to repeat my habitual "mantras" over and over in my head or under my breath to keep away the evil. The horrific images were the most prevalent and the worst to deal with. I had to uncontrollably "make" myself visualize outrageously disturbing things happening to those about whom I cared the most.

I had all *kinds* of rituals. They, like the rest of my OCD symptoms, totally filled my days, exhausting me from the moment I awoke until the time I finally attempted to escape into sleep. A few of them involved mirrors, watches, numbers and counting, all to take the "magic" out of my fear of harming others. For about a year I was unable to work, but when I *could* work, I constantly corrected the work I had done. My work was a stressful mess, to say the least.

To backtrack, I'll briefly describe my experience with

Tourette's syndrome. I had a terrible fear of feeling relief; real pleasure was even worse. I was afraid that if I "let go" all the bad feelings, thoughts or images would get out and into the real world. Now, I knew this was ridiculous, but to keep it all in I blinked, twitched and contorted my face. I grunted and clicked my tongue, contorted my breathing and maneuvered my arms – I was in hell.

My drug addiction led me to a methadone maintenance program by the time I found out exactly what I had. I saw a talk show about my disease and the word was that a book *The Boy Who Couldn't Stop Washing,* by Dr. Judith L. Rapoport, was due to be released soon. Reading that book was one of the most touching experiences of my life. I found out that I was not alone. Not only that, but I discovered that I was not even *unusual* for a person with OCD, and that we are not even that uncommon in society. It was a revelation for me.

I wanted to get *better.* My addiction was being steadied by the methadone while I was in the long process of detoxification, but I was powerless to really stop my course and I didn't know it. I didn't know that there was an answer out there. Then I met up with A.A. again. This time someone *absolutely insisted* that I take a Big Book home with me.

After that meeting I read the book and I saw the answer to my problem. Yes, the solution to my alcoholism and drug problem was there, but most certainly there also lay my answer to my insanity with OCD and Tourette's syndrome.

I believed in a loving God my whole life, and deep down I had known that a trust in Him was my only hope, but I had no tools to accomplish this trust.

I believe that our disease, like alcoholism, is a disease of self-centeredness. Getting involved in trying to meet the needs of others is where recovery has been for me, an ability that has only been made possible through the Twelve Steps. It has been something that has taken time to become reality, but today it pervades my entire life. It must or I suffer again.

I knew about OCA during most of my sobriety and had wanted to start a meeting here in Los Angeles, but for a long time I had to concentrate on my recovery through the steps. I applied the steps to my OCD/Tourette's *from the very beginning.* When the time came to apply the twelfth step, and I felt that I had enough experience to warrant it, I was ready to start an OCA group in LA. A chance meeting with a fellow A.A. with OCD started the process. Our meeting is flourishing; so far three people have asked me to sponsor them. This sponsorship is part of *my* recovery as well as theirs.

Today I live a joyful, useful life. There are tough moments, but this program has shown me how to put one foot in front of the other and to walk through it — on the road to happy destiny.

May God bless you.

(29)
OCD No Longer Has Me

Sunday, June 21, 1992, was my two-year anniversary in OCA. If I was there with you I would lead a meeting and share my story – my experience, strength and hope – as a way of celebrating my anniversary. Even though I'm far away, I must celebrate in some way because that day two years ago when I first went to an OCA meeting is the most important day of my life and the beginning of my recovery from this bitch of a disease, OCD.

I write for myself tonight because a small obsession is going in my head and tonight I'll do what has worked for me, one day at a time to be free from OCD: I work the steps and I work the program. Since I have a small obsession tonight, you know that I am not cured of OCD, but I do have a daily reprieve from it based on maintaining a simple spiritual adherence to the program – going to meetings, reading literature, calling my sponsor, working on the steps, making phone calls (writing letters!) or praying – taking action to maintain my recovery. I do have recovery today, an unbelievable, incredible amount, for which I am so grateful.

I am a handwasher. I began washing my hands uncontrollably at age twelve, as well as washing objects in my environment and living in obsessions about dirt and contamination. Prior to entering OCA I washed my hands seventy times a day, sometimes spending as long as a half hour at a sink washing my arms beyond my elbows. Showers too were one of my favorite places; I have spent, many torturous hours in the shower, not being able to come out until I was right and clean in OCD terms.

From my very first OCA meeting I began to feel peace and relief from my disease, a peace and release from OCD I had never before experienced and which I had never been able to fabricate myself, try as I did for twelve years. Counseling and other treatments for my bizarre behavior, which I did not understand and which I felt uncontrollably compelled to do, never put a dent in my OCD. OCA, the program and the Twelve Steps, have not only put a dent in my OCD, it has removed me from the horrible, painful bondage of OCD. OCA has removed the power of my obsession and my compulsive behavior.

After less than a year in the program I noticed that in a period of one week, simply by working the program one day at a time, I had only washed my hands seven times. Since I have returned from a Twelve Step recovery treatment program for addictions and compulsive behaviors, I have not run to the sink to wash my hands (for solely an OCD reason) and I have not stood chained to the sink at all. Today, the sink, water and soap have no power over me, but that's because I'm power*less* over my OCD.

As I write about the last seven months of my life, it sounds like my recovery has come about so easily. But nothing is further from the truth. The past months of freedom from my OCD are actually only many, many one-day-at-a-times put together. Much of it has been a minute at a time. Today I did not wash or act obsessively, which is an incredible miracle in my life.

The OCD thoughts still come and go, but that's *all* they do; they come and they go rather quickly. As a good friend of mine in OCA says, "Today I have OCD, but OCD doesn't have me." The miracle of living without compulsive washing has not been just handed to me as a simple cure, but has come through a lot of program action and working the steps. It has come through being willing to go to any lengths, through prayer, attending meetings, picking up the phone (even when I didn't want to), twelfth-step work, long talks each day with my sponsor, surrender and letting go, and most of all, through conscious contact with my Higher Power. I have done the footwork, but I did not give myself the peace and serenity I feel tonight. That has been a gift I received from my first day in OCA and which I know could only come from some power greater than myself. Today I have a very real relationship with this Higher Power and without it I would be lost.

OCA is my lifeline. All of you recovering from OCD with me give me support, strength and hope. I am so incredibly grateful for my recovery from OCD and I am equally, if not more, grateful for all of you because without you, without OCA, I could never have the peace, serenity and recovery I have tonight. This is most definitely a "we" program – no matter if we meet together weekly or are recovering four hundred miles apart.

I wish you all peace and serenity today and continued recovery, and I thank you. Keep working the program; I don't know why it works – I just know that it does.

Love and peace and happy second anniversary in OCA to me.

Obsessive Compulsive Anonymous

(30)
Blessings in Disguise

Although I certainly can't say I felt lucky when OCD made its ugly re-entrance into my life less than a year ago, I've since realized how lucky I am that the right doctors, therapists, medications, friends and book fell onto my path at the right time.

My OCD presented itself as anxiety attacks. My career was going well, my two year marriage was growing stronger each day, my family wasn't facing any crisis, and yet, without warning, the confidence I had enjoyed for most of my life vanished, leaving me a clinging, helpless child, convinced that doom was just around the corner.

I had only two misdiagnoses: first, some doctors thought I was having a toxic reaction to a prescription decongestant; next they tested me for thyroid problems. I've come to realize that getting only two misdiagnoses is rare – and lucky – in the realm of anxiety disorders and OCD. It took less than a month for the latest doctor I saw to send me to a psychiatrist. My family, not the most psychologically oriented bunch you'll find, was surprisingly and gratifyingly supportive. Still, I wasn't convinced that anything was really wrong with me until my life began to change a little each day. Soon I was no longer able to keep up with the most routine activities, like going to work, staying by myself, spending time at home, eating, cooking or sleeping through the night. The low point occurred during the week in which I drove my husband to work (although his office is in the opposite direction from my own) before driving to work. I was afraid to let him drive for fear he would die in a car accident.

Then there were days when I couldn't go to my office at all. I couldn't stay at home by myself either, so my husband and I would pack off to his office where I would sit by his side, terrified, angry at myself and mortified to endure the curious glances from his well-meaning but uninformed coworkers.

The breakthrough came one day in therapy when I asked my psychiatrist if everyone had trouble "turning off" their thoughts at times when they should be able to mentally rest. From there, she keyed in on my OCD characteristics and my improvement began.

There are those who believe OCD is wholly biochemical in cause. In my case though, I think the biochemical predisposition was fueled by events in my emotional development. My earliest OCD memories are of being three years old and fighting for control in inherently uncontrollable situations. When I was three my mother had to leave town to attend my grandmother's funeral. I was too young to comprehend death, but I got a taste of the finality of it, somehow confused the situation and believed my mother had died and was not coming back. When she did return, I was afraid to let her out of my sight again and I became inconsolable if she would even leave the room.

Eventually my fears calmed to a tolerable level, but they returned with an awful OCD twist when I started school. My mother, who drove me to school, is always late. Each time I stood outside of the school waiting for her at the end of the day, my mind would not let me recognize this fact, but convinced me that something terrible had happened to her. She was never coming back. I gradually slipped into coping mechanisms, OCD thoughts, really, that gave me an illusion of being able to control my mother's safety. For example, if I didn't go to the bathroom all day, or didn't step on any cracks in the sidewalk, or held my breath to the count of twenty, nothing would happen to her.

Years later, when my anxiety attacks began, I found myself

incorporating the same kind of "magic thinking" into my life, but now with my husband as the focus. If I wore a pair of earrings he had given me (even if they didn't particularly match my outfit), I believed he'd be safe. If I didn't wear those earrings, he would not be OK and it would all be my fault.

As my therapy progressed and the second drug I was prescribed began to help, I got the final nudge on my shoulder from God. While browsing in a bookstore, I found myself inexplicably drawn to the self-help section. In the back of my mind I remembered my therapist saying that a Twelve Step program could help me and I was looking for some kind of general guidance on the subject. It took fewer than two minutes to find *OCA: Recovering from Obsessive-Compulsive Disorder.* I tore through that book that night, drawing comfort from the knowledge that there were others out there who had walked through my pain.

The next day I found out about an OCA meeting in my area. The final pieces of my recovery began that night when I shared the fellowship of others who finally truly understood and empathized. It is one thing to receive reassurance from a professional therapist, but quite another to look across the table at someone who looks quite "normal" and hear them say the things that I have been thinking. I was amazed to find people who had the same OCD "quirks" as me − "typing" words with my fingers as people talk and counting the number of swallows I take from a drink. At OCA I began to understand that OCD did not have to cripple me. I was soon able to let my husband drive alone to work and I was surprised at the relief I felt when I quit making the two-and a-half-hour commute each day. Eventually I even stayed home by myself without anxiety.

Many times it's hard to see that blessings can come from OCD. I'm the original skeptic. I hated the way it had taken over so many parts of my life. But as I've realized that I don't have to control everything, I've seen the many ways in which I have been blessed. Thanks to the recent publicity and education about OCD from groups like OCA, the doctors I saw were able to diagnose my problem and start me on the recovery process quickly.

From my experience with OCD I have a newfound sympathy and patience for people with emotional problems. OCA restored my faith in God and other people, and helped bring me back to church. I needed help and I turned to groups of strangers (in AlAnon and OCA) who met my fears with open arms and willing ears. I know I am blessed because when I was unsure of myself and the reception that awaited me, they welcomed me in, "quirks" and all.

(31)
I'm a Human Being

I'm twenty-two years old and I have OCD. My symptoms probably started when I was about nine years old, but I could actually have had OCD much earlier than that. When I was growing up I never felt like the other kids. I always felt as though I was in my own world and alone. There truly *were* problems in my family, including compulsive gambling and alcoholism, which most likely play a part in my having obsessive compulsive disorder.

I guess I could say that my two biggest obsessions were checking and getting "stuck" on something. Actually it seems like I've obsessed about everything. Although I couldn't name them all, my obsessions and compulsions included lucky and unlucky numbers, contamination fears, my personal appearance, checking doors and ovens, and my clothing.

At about the age of sixteen, I finally confessed these fears to my parents. My father told me I would grow out of them. Well, this wasn't true; it just got worse after high school. I went to college for three years and then quit both school and my part-time job to start my career. At that point I guess the OCD knew what I was trying to do because I became a total wreck. It seems the OCD doesn't like change!

I was so drained from the OCD that I could barely breathe. I just wanted to quit everything and drop out of life completely. I was seriously contemplating suicide until my mother told me about OCA. At first I didn't want to go to meetings, but I knew I was dying from this disorder ... therefore *I must go.*

I joined the program and followed what was suggested. My life has completely turned around. Today I'm facing my worst fears and have a new outlook on life. Honestly, this program is no joke! I believe this program is going to help so many people in the future.

Basically, when I did my praying, meditating and reading, I felt my Higher Power, which I call God, working – something happened. I felt a source of energy beyond belief. It's like believing in the unbelievable.

For a while I couldn't really figure out the best thing that the program offers me. Is it that I'm more self-confident, I manage my money better, I'm more organized, I enjoy living or that I have a highly responsible job? Then it hit me – it's none of those. What it is that for the first time I feel like a human being instead of something with a rope around its neck being pulled by someone everywhere it goes. I'm truly grateful to this program. Well, good luck!

(32)
Hangups

I am a "pure-O" – as in obsessive. I've always referred to my obsessions as "hangups," although they are called different names by different sufferers: "scruples," "my stuff," "quirks," and "spikes," to mention a few. The bottom line is, regardless of the label, hangups can demolish us.

I'm not exclusively an obsessive though. I have managed to mix in a lot of meaningless, ritualistic compulsions. Looking back, I think they were a form of insurance against acquiring future hangups. My hangups were always viciously painful, never affording even a crumb of pleasure. At least alcoholics, sex addicts and overeaters can initially derive physical pleasure from their disorders.

I was raised in a loving, *functional* home with extremely supportive parents. I want to emphasize the operative word *functional* in order to counter the popular notion that only members of dysfunctional families end up in Twelve Step programs. I don't recall having any obsessions as a young child, although I always felt I was not as good as others. I also recall that superstitions were more real and frightening to me than to most children.

At five years of age I was deathly afraid of germs. I washed my hands a lot. One day I ran up to my grandmother exclaiming that I had eaten a piece of candy that had dropped on the floor and asked her if I would die. I'll never forget her comforting words, "Oh, dear, of course not. Everyone has to eat a bushel of dirt before they die!" Today I'm sure the "environmentally correct" would shudder at such an adage, but it calmed me instantly. I validated life through my parents and grandparents. I think had it not been for my dear grandmother, I might have become a compulsive handwasher. Instead I took off the other way and became something of a slob.

My first hangup occurred when I was about twelve years old. My middle brother and I were watching "Spin and Marty" on TV. I asked him if one of the characters was Spin. He answered, "Yes." Then I continued to ask, "Huh?" several more times, even though I had heard him clearly the first time. Something inside me compelled me to keep on asking until it felt "right." Sometimes he would staunchly refuse to answer, at which times I twisted the poor little guy's arm or hit him until he acceded to my dictates. I'm not proud of such behavior, but at the time I thought all kinds of horrors might happen if he didn't keep answering me. I might go blind, suffer castration or lose a loved one. I knew these things probably would never really happen, yet I was compelled to give them serious consideration. I really felt weird.

As my teen years rolled by, so did the severity of those hangups. One hangup devastated me for seven long years: How could I be sure that I would never, ever throw my little ten-year-old brother (whom I dearly loved) off the top floor of a particular downtown parking garage? I didn't think I would ever resolve this hangup. It was horrible beyond belief. After I finally did resolve it, I had a respite from ruminating for less than a day.

Then a new thought popped into my mind which hung me up for two more years. I felt helpless to stop it. The pattern was that a seemingly unsolvable thought would bug me, taking all of my concentration and shutting out the rest of the world in the process. I'm sure I hurt my family and friends very deeply. I have tried to make amends.

At times, if I could muster the courage, I shared my hangups with a few friends. However, they just shrugged them off as trivial, offering reassurances like "It's no big deal," or

"Just forget about it." Such feedback made me feel even worse because then I felt guilty for worrying about something that wasn't important.

During those horrible times I managed to function, albeit below my potential. I often wondered how much better I would perform in life in general if not for the hangups on my back. I graduated from Ohio State University and went on to obtain my masters degree in architecture from Columbia University. Throughout my ordeal, architecture was one of the few positive constants in my life. It has always been a great passion. I'd often wonder how much better I might be at it without the needless compulsions, such as retaping my paper down on my drafting table a certain number of times. With such irrational, not to mention costly, behavior to my bosses I didn't hold jobs for very long.

I also served as a combat infantryman with Oliver Stone in Vietnam. Stone based the movie *Platoon* on our unit's experiences. In fact, Stone and I were shot at during an ambush, which he later depicted in the movie. I point this out to illustrate that even an enemy ambush couldn't scare the hangup out of me. At the time of the ambush I was still obsessing about my brother and the parking garage.

I could go on and on about my hangups, which involved diverse things such as counting, sex, color combinations, words, certain rhythms and forgetting a train of thought. If I forgot a train of thought, it might be the worst possible thought to forget! Usually, after considerable ruminating, I remembered it. It would be wonderful, like the "Aha!" phenomena. I could breathe again for a bit, until the next hangup.

During my years as a practicing OCD sufferer, about the only relief was alcohol. Treatment for OCD was virtually nonexistent in the early 70s. I did go to a psychiatrist as a last resort in 1974. I hated the idea of going crazy; I felt seeking help from a psychiatrist would validate my suspicion, but I couldn't take it anymore. I spilled my guts out for an hour. As I left, the psychiatrist said I might benefit from further treatment but, "quite frankly, you do not earn enough money and your condition is probably just a mild form of depression."

So I drank. I developed a tremendous tolerance for alcohol, but did not know I was an alcoholic. In 1975, I found myself in trouble with the law for intoxication, disorderly conduct and resisting arrest. The judge offered me a choice: A.A. or jail. I took A.A. and something "took" me. All I did was bring my frail body and foggy mind to the meetings and something magical happened. I had a spiritual awakening. At the time I was an atheist, although I had been raised in a religious family. This, however, had nothing to do with religion; this was spiritual. The strength that I got helped me not only with my alcohol problems, but also with my obsessions. I simply internalized the Twelve Step recovery program of A.A. to help me with my hangups by substituting the word "hangups" for "alcohol" in the steps. I celebrated life two or three times a day at meetings, wearing my two hats — alcoholic and obsessive.

One of my brothers also started going to meetings and using the Twelve Step program for both disorders. Today he and I have more than sixteen years of continuous sobriety/OCD recovery. At times there have been disturbing contradictions between the two programs. For example, in A.A. one is often reminded that alcoholics tend to blame others for their problems. However, for my hangups, I always pointed the accusing finger at myself. Also in A.A. we are taught that we can only change ourselves and should stop trying to change others; if only I could have changed myself! God only knows I tried hard enough. But in spite of such contradictions, A.A. has worked for me because – of my conscious contact with my Higher Power. However, one day it dawned on me that there are OCD sufferers who are not recovering alcoholics who are obviously missing the boat. So in 1988 my brother and I founded Obsessives Anonymous in Ohio. Since pure obsessives became difficult to find, I am now devoting my full effort to our OCA group, which my brother and I founded in Columbus in 1990.

While OCD is and always will be a part of me, the frequency and severity of my obsessions are relatively mild. I would certainly take medication for my disorder if I felt I needed to, but so far I haven't, one day at a time. Life is not only tolerable, it is actually fun. My worst day in recovery is better than my best day obsessing. Instead of throwing all the "cherries" in life away and keeping all the "crap," today I'm able to reverse the order. Now when a threatening hangup pops into my conscious mind, I know how to deal with it: I turn it over using the third step. Sometimes I still wrestle with hangups a bit. I don't always turn them over effortlessly. But I do know that my Higher Power will never give me more ruminating than I can handle.

Today I have a wonderful mate, an improving relationship with my daughter, the best parents a guy could have and my youngest brother, my running buddy in A.A./OCA. Even my middle brother and I get along better. I have had an architectural career at the same place for sixteen years (a miracle). I also have the desire to reach out and help others. Being the OCA contact person in Columbus has immeasurably enriched my life. Only another person with OCD can really know what it's like to have the disease. It's wonderful to know that I'm not alone. In closing I'll part with a quote by Robert Ardrey: "There is nothing so moving – not even acts of love or hate – as the discovery that one is not alone."

(33)
Pain in My Mind's Eye

I don't really know when my OCD began, but I do know that it has taken on many forms over the years. When I was very young, approximately age six, I had a compulsion to twist my hair, which I did until I had a bald spot on top of my head. I also remember having to arrange my toys in a certain way or else I would become very anxious. At age thirteen my OCD began to become a problem. I was teased constantly about how ugly and inept I was, so I eventually began to doubt all of my abilities.

At this time I became a "checker." I was compelled to check all switches and faucets to make sure they were off. I had to unplug all small appliances and recheck locked doors. At school I was always the last person to turn in my answer sheets because I had to check my answers on tests again and again. The worst part of this was no matter how many times I checked, I was still convinced something bad was going to happen. I didn't trust my sense; my eyes told me everything was fine, but my mind refused to be convinced.

I somehow made it to high school. At this time my checking compulsion subsided, but OCD gave me other things to think about. I was convinced that other people were better looking than me, so I became very obsessed with my looks and what people thought about me. My clothes, hair and actions all had to be perfect. As if this wasn't enough, I was certain that I would not perform well in a relationship with a woman, so I avoided getting close to anybody. I was able to go out on dates, but was sure I would do something wrong and the girl wouldn't like me anymore.

I cannot tell you how painful all this was. It was like constantly walking in a minefield and not knowing when there would be an explosion.

In high school I discovered that I liked woodworking. This was a consolation because I loved making things; however, my OCD began to intervene here too. I had to double-check clamps and screws, and when I was done, I constantly berated myself because my project had some minor flaws. Even if the flaws could not be seen, I felt compelled to rework it again and again until it was perfect.

After high school I continued on to a local junior college. My avoidance of relationships and my perfectionism continued, but I channeled my energies into my studies and achieved an excellent grade point average. After receiving my two-year degree, I made a decision to move away from home and transfer to a four-year university. This major change filled me with anxiety and my checking compulsion returned with a vengeance.

Whenever I left my mobile home I went through a strict routine of checking from one end of the trailer to the other. I knew that if I didn't do this, something would be left on and my house would burn down and kill someone. I spent three hours or longer checking everything before I could leave. Then, after finally locking the door and going out to my car, I would invariably have to go back and check something else, all the while feeling like a fool.

The checking also showed up in my driving. If I passed somebody walking on the side of the road, I became convinced that I had run that person over and I would have to go back and check. This compulsion became so bad, I began to ride my bicycle everywhere except for long-distance trips.

I somehow made it through college and became employed with a construction firm as an assistant superintendent on a power plant project. One of my tasks was to act as a quality control inspector, which opened up all kinds of checking possibilities for someone like me. I had to check the plans, the forms and the reinforcing steel endlessly. Even after all that work, I woke up at night, thinking of something I had forgotten and worrying about the building falling down and killing someone. A picture of death and destruction played over and over in my mind's eye.

After eight months of pure hell on this job, I quit and went back home. I found a job as a carpenter and my OCD subsided. When I accepted a position supervising home construction, my checking compulsion started all over again and I quit in a deep depression. During that time of unemployment, I slept almost all of the time because it was my only escape from the torturous thoughts. I was scared to get a new job because I was sure it would be the same as before.

I also became obsessed with cleanliness and order during this period. I spent hours cleaning the house and organizing my possessions. I became very angry when anyone made a mess and didn't care enough to clean it up. Finally, after I had a serious argument with my mother, my sister convinced me to get a job and some help.

I finally gained enough courage to accept a sales position at a local retailer. This allowed me to work without all the worries brought on by construction.

My recovery from OCD began in a place I least expected. I was reading the newspaper and found an advertisement for an organization called OCA. I phoned and found out they met every Tuesday night. I started going to meetings, at first very skeptical that it would help me, but I soon discovered that people in the group understood the fear, the loneliness and the pain this disorder brings. Simply being able to talk to someone who has been through the same things as I have helped immensely.

As I began to work the Steps, I found courage that I never had before. I was able to find a new job, enter into relationships with less fear and discuss any problem I was having without worrying that people would think I was stupid. What's even more unbelievable is I have done all this and I am only on the third step in the program

My best advice to those new to the program is to keep coming back to the meetings and give our program a chance to work. No one was more skeptical than me, but I refused to give up on the program and I've benefited greatly. Also, get as much information on OCD as is available. Go to the library, read books, magazines, newspapers and anything which has information on OCD. Just becoming more informed about the disorder and realizing you are not alone will help immensely. My last piece of advice is to talk, talk, talk. Don't be afraid to tell people how you feel because this is the key to recovery; you talk about your feelings and in return, you receive input and strength from others and the program. Another benefit of the program is the ability to help others. I've found that my recovery has progressed more rapidly by helping others cope with OCD.

I have great hopes for the future because I am convinced that my recovery lies in OCA and the Twelve Steps. I am still struggling with resistance to change, striving to be perfect, urges to check and avoidance of relationships; however, I know that with God's help and the program, the good times will vastly outnumber the bad ones.

To Our Families and Friends

Until now, most of the literature on OCD has focused on the individual with "the problem." Rarely has mention been made of the family and friends who love and/or live with a person with OCD. Often these families suffer greatly along with the person with OCD. Our message here is to help families recover from the battleground of OCD even if their loved ones don't get better.

A family member may be thinking right now, "How can I enjoy my life, especially if my loved one is still suffering with OCD?" Much of family time might be spent fighting with OCD with little time left for the family. Many families, in an attempt to "keep the peace," have completed rituals for the individual with OCD or have answered obsessive questions repeatedly. Or, perhaps anger entered into the picture as the family member screamed at the person with OCD to "JUST STOP!" These responses are not effective against OCD and just escalate anxiety for everyone involved.

The AlAnon program, created in response to alcoholism, has developed three simple principles which can be applied to OCD:

1) The family didn't *cause* OCD.

2) The family can't *control* OCD.

3) The family can't *cure* OCD.

At first these principles may seem radical to someone trying to "get control" or "stay on top" of painful situations caused by another's OCD. But these simple statements (the "Three C's") allow families to distance themselves from the illness and to unload the accumulated guilt.

As many people know, there are several treatments for OCD today – behavior therapy, medications and support groups like OCA. Families can show their loved ones where this help is available, but it is up to the person with OCD to actually try these options. The family cannot force anyone to work on their recovery – in general, the person with OCD has to be willing to do the work.

Family members can find it shocking to see the person with OCD reluctant to try these options despite his or her obvious suffering. If this is the case, it is imperative that the family doesn't "enable" the person with OCD. In terms of OCD, enabling means protecting someone from the consequences of his or her illness. It is not the family's responsibility to make excuses for someone who is late due to OCD. It is important not to attempt to make the environment "OCD free" nor to disrupt the family's normal routine to satisfy OCD rituals. Instead, the AlAnon principle of "detaching with love" allows family members to love the person while pulling away from his or her disease.

Now about family dynamics. Years spent with OCD take their toll on families. Unhappy patterns develop and a healthy two-way relationship proves impossible over time. Usually the person with OCD "shuts down" emotionally while simultaneously relying on the family for his or her most basic needs. This inability to form a natural give-and-take relationship can lock a family into a "comfortable misery" with little chance for change. The solution is to shift the focus from the illness and onto taking care of oneself. All of the family members are entitled to time for themselves, which can include activities long ago abandoned for the OCD.

Additionally, families can find it helpful to try the Twelve Steps which so many have found to be a bridge back to life. These steps help people to see things honestly and, most important, let them recognize how they each have contributed to the disharmony in the household. While families don't cause OCD, there seem to be certain personality traits present in families with a member with OCD. Family members need to acknowledge control issues which do not allow individual freedom and desires to be expressed. Also, perfectionism and impossibly high standards tend to fuel OCD symptoms. A family consumed with fear, in which everything is a crisis, certainly makes healing difficult. Excessive anger and blaming others for OCD also lead nowhere. In the Twelve Steps these issues are addressed and changes can be made. Some find the discussion of a "Higher Power" in the steps to be a stumbling block, but the steps are only suggestions – no one is trying to make family members or friends believe in anything.

About the child whose parent or parents have OCD: Although these children may not develop OCD, they will often bear other scars. Rigid rules and unrealistic expectations were the norm in their childhood. A parent's struggle for control limits a child's freedom of choice. Often feelings of being trapped in the parent's cycle of illness develop. Doing things outside the family "boundaries" results in guilt, so little was done to change the status quo. *As adults in recovery these people learn to nurture their own needs as opposed to nurturing their parents' needs for control.* This recovery for adult children of obsessive compulsives also lies in detachment from OCD; support and guidance can be found in therapy, in the Twelve-Step program of OC-Anon or other groups.

As for the family whose member has found Obsessive Compulsive Anonymous, Be patient! This approach works on an individual time schedule. If your loved one has found OCA and intends to give it his or her best shot, recovery is likely. Let him or her spend as much time as he or she responsibly can in meetings or working the program. Try not to feel jealous of his or her attention to OCA; this is how the fellowship works. Enthusiasm will help the obsessive-compulsive to recover as he or she is willing to work the program diligently.

Remembering that no one is responsible for another's recovery is essential. We are only responsible for our own recovery program.

These suggestions will, we hope, help make life a bit easier and a relationship with the person with OCD more rewarding. To receive a copy of our book, *Obsessive Compulsive Disorder – A Survival Guide for Family and Friends*, which addresses these issues, send $10.00 (US dollars/US bank) per book to:

Obsessive Compulsive Anonymous World Services
Box 215
New Hyde Park, NY 11040

Remember to include your address with your check or money order. Shipping costs are included for the USA and Canada – outside areas add actual shipping costs.

Some Helpful Suggestions

1. - We utilize the program – not analyze it. The reasons why it works for us are not important – *what is important is that it works.*

2. - This is a "we" program – by attending meetings and getting active in OCA we recover together.

3. - At our meetings we emphasize our application of the 12 Step program to reduce our OCD. OCA is *not* a place to endlessly discuss our obsessions and compulsions. We *are* gathered to share our common *solution* to this problem – the 12 Step program.

4. - *Recovery* through OCA is defined as the relief obtained from our obsessions and compulsions as a result of working the 12 Step program. "Total abstinence" from OCD is *not* our focus – instead we focus on our daily application of program and its incorporation into our lives. This emphasis will result in a reduction of OCD symptoms and a state of well-being.

5. - OCA is not a psychological counseling service nor do we make medical referrals. For information in those areas call the OC Foundation

6. - Outside treatments for OCD are just that – outside treatments. We do not endorse or oppose specific outside treatments for OCD. We have found that those of us who are receiving medical or psychological treatments for OCD can work this program with good results. We ask our members not to discuss these treatments during our meetings. At OCA our focus is on the 12 Step program and how we use it to gain relief from our OCD.

7. - We have found it helpful not to evaluate anyone's illness

or recovery. *We recommend those struggling with the program to keep coming back to give our way of life a chance to work for them.*

8. - We use the "tools" of the program to recover – the 12 Steps, meetings and fellowship – Our Higher Power works through these avenues.

9. - Sponsorship aids us in our recovery. We can't recover alone – our sponsors can provide a better working understanding of the program.

10.- *Knowledge* about the inner workings of our OCD *does not* produce recovery. Our program doesn't address why we got our particular "brand" of OCD – it addresses how to recover from it.

11.- Our change in attitude results in our change in OCD. We need to be open to program suggestions so we can make the necessary changes in our lives for recovery.

12.- Working with newcomers is the backbone of our recovery. We stay well by spreading our recovery program.

Some Helpless Suggestions –
Or What <u>Doesn't</u> Work in OCA

1. Please decide after only a few meetings that OCA cannot help you and your "unique OCD problems."

2. Don't forget to criticize and judge everyone at the meetings.

3. Consistently complain about your OCD and other life situations, and look no further than yourself for your answers.

4. Don't forget to come late and leave early at meetings, and try not to listen while you're there.

5. Listen to the OCA members who say that the spiritual side of the program is unimportant and ignore the Twelve Steps in their entirety.

6. Don't forget to take more than you give in OCA, and in life in general.

7. Hold on tightly to resentments and life's inequities while there's still time.

8. Please discuss at length matters entirely unrelated to the meeting's topic, and don't forget to whine and focus in on the negative.

9. Make sure your OCA program is full of non-OCA material and share this information at every meeting.

10. Please cross-talk when others are speaking, and when necessary, correct them.

11. Don't forget to over-discuss your OCD symptoms and please ignore the feelings/issues that fuel them.

12. Change as little as possible and be careful not to follow the suggestions of those who have recovery.

13. Please work the "Thirteenth Step" as often as possible, paying special attention to those vulnerable newcomers who might "need" a date with you.

SLOGANS

Worry is failure to trust

FEAR stands for Face Everything And Recover
False Events Appearing Real

Good enough is good enough

The power is in the moment

Attitude is a little thing that makes a big difference

In recovery I may have OCD, but OCD no longer has me

The world won't get better because you joined OCA – but
you will

Avoid the PLOMS – Poor Little Old Me's

HALT – Don't get too Hungry, Angry, Lonely or Tired

Fear is the darkroom where negatives are developed

If God seems far away – Who moved?

Live life on life's terms

OCA is easy – All you have to do is come to meetings, and
change your whole life

Seven days without a meeting makes one weak

Stick with the winners

Be part of the solution – don't live in the problem

Four A's – Acceptance, Awareness, Action, Attitude

Let Go and Let God

Put some gratitude in your attitude

HOW – Honesty, Open-mindedness, Willingness

God never gives us more than we can handle – but he always
gives us more than we can control

If we keep one foot in yesterday and the other foot in tomorrow we piss on today

Act – don't react

If nothing changes – nothing changes

Don't analyze – utilize

What someone else is thinking of me is really none of my business

Disagree without being disagreeable

We are responsible for the effort – not the results

Procrastination only results in keeping up with yesterday

EGO – Ease God Out

Recovery from OCD is not thinking less of yourself – but thinking of yourself less

Easy Does It – But Do It

GOD – Good Orderly Direction

A path with no obstacles surely leads nowhere

OCA isn't for those who need it – it's for those who want it

OCA works if you work it – it won't if you don't

We want to be exceptional, but fear we are not even adequate

Take what you need and leave the rest

Trying to pray *is* praying

There are none too dumb for OCA, but many who are too smart

We can act ourselves into right thinking more easily than we can think ourselves into right acting

People with OCD don't form relationships – we take hostages

A person who is aiming at nothing has a target he can't miss

Things turn out the best for people who make the best of the way things turn out

Stick with the winners – win with the stickers

Those having trouble "with the program" are usually having trouble without the program

Self-centered people become so wrapped up in themselves that they become very small packages

Self-pity is like a dirty diaper – first we take some comfort but eventually it begins to stink

One day at a time

First things first

Turn it over

Too much analyzing leads to paralyzing

Live and Let Live

Perfectionism ➜ Procrastination ➜ Paralyzation

KISS – Keep It Simple, Sweetie

Feelings aren't always facts

This too shall pass

Identify; don't compare

Progress not perfection

Don't "should" on yourself

The most important things in life aren't things

Anger is fear turned inward

There is not a spot, where God is not

Our enemies are often our greatest teachers

A man cannot be at peace with others, until he is at peace with himself

An apology is a great way to have the last word in an argument

If you worry about what might be and wonder what might have been, you will miss what is

When you blame others, you give up your power to change

Pain may be inevitable – but misery is optional

Cluttering up our minds with the little things leaves no room for the big things

Worry is interest paid on trouble before it is due

Serenity is not the absence of conflict but the ability to cope with it

You can't heal what you can't feel

When you don't want a meeting is when you need one most

Don't compare your insides to someone else's outsides

People who are ill with OCD are not "out of their minds,"– they just spend too much time "in their minds"

Never give it a <u>THIRD</u> thought

The squeaky wheel doesn't always get the oil – sometimes it gets replaced!

Trust God – "Clean House" – Help Others

You only get as much out of OCA as you put in

Instead of "picking up" your OCD – pick up the phone

When given a "lemon" – make "lemonade"

When I first got to OCA the meetings were "crazy"– now that I've been coming awhile they have remained "crazy"– but I'm getting better!

People with OCD won't notice an elephant on their own head, but will point out a fly on someone else's

Say what you mean, mean what you say, but don't say it mean

If I row, God will steer

OCA is like a raffle, you must be present to win

Harboring a resentment is just like injecting a poison – and waiting for someone else to die

Put down your weapons and pick up the tools

The only real closure in life is death

A possibility doesn't equal a probability

What you do speaks so loudly that what you say can't be heard

Not everything has to be done today. When you die your in – basket will still be full

My head is like a bad neighborhood – I try not to go there alone

I don't know for sure if I have OCD – I just have all the symptoms

S.M.A.R.T. Steps Meetings Acceptance Risk-taking Trust

Work as if everything depends on you. Pray as if everything depends on God.

Rigorous honesty doesn't mean rigid honesty

Don't pray like a teabag – only when you're in hot water

G.A.N.E. GOD ACCEPTANCE NOT ENGAGE

Be a "20/20" meeting person – come 20 minutes before and stay 20 minutes after the meeting

How to make God laugh – MAKE PLANS

With obsessions RESIST = PERSIST

The only "tools" in OCA you pay for are the ones you don't use.

Today is the tomorrow you worried about yesterday

We're only as sick as our secrets

"No" is a complete sentence

Be careful what you pray for – you might get it

When confronted with an obsession – do what the "average" person would do!

TOOLS

These are tools that we have found which aid us in implementing the Twelve Steps into our lives. We have found that if we are willing to take the following actions, marvelous things start to occur in our lives.

1 . A commitment to ABSTINENCE: letting go of obsessive thoughts and not completing OCD rituals. With this commitment, we are able to find an ease in practicing the principles of Step One.

2. SPONSORSHIP: As the very foundation of our program is one helping another, we ask someone to guide us through the journey of recovery. Sponsors are those who are committed to the practice and principles of the Twelve Steps in all their affairs.

3. MEETINGS: Attendance at meetings enables us to identify, experience and share those feelings which we have repressed with our OCD. By hearing others open up, we are more able to find the willingness to be more honest, and freer in our pursuits.

4. The TELEPHONE: provides us with a mini meeting. Again, it is an opportunity to help one another – the essence of the Twelve Steps – Please do not hesitate: CALL!

6. LITERATURE: is used as a guide to our program of recovery. Twelve Step literature from other programs is also helpful.

7. SERVICE: is a many-faceted tool. Service provides us with the means of freeing ourselves from nagging obsessions. It is a means of getting out of one's self and giving back to OCA a little of what we have received. Service may be in the form of a commitment, or volunteering on the spot, such as setting up, cleaning up, making coffee, holding an office, leading or speaking at meetings, giving a ride, welcoming and talking to newcomers, or by " carrying the message" to the person who still suffers from OCD. By doing service we are able to see the light of the Twelfth Step.

What is an OCA Meeting Like?

A healing occurs in our meetings which seems to defy explanation. If you are a member of another Twelve Step program you are already familiar with "program" meetings. The following are OCA's suggestions for a meeting format:

OPENING

Welcome to the _____ (day of the week) meeting of Obsessive Compulsive Anonymous. My name is _____ and I'm your chairperson for this meeting. This is a rotating meeting, which means we use a different focus each week, rotating between step, story, qualification and topic. Today's focus is _____ (step, story, qualification or topic). _____ is defined as: [choose appropriate definition: *step* – our current relation to, or progress in today's step as described in OCA literature; *story* our feelings about or reflections on a story from OCA literature; a *qualification* in which _____ (name) will share his or her experience, strength and hope with us, followed by sharing; the *topic* is a relevant issue, problem, solution or common emotion pertaining to OCD recovery, to be addressed first by the speaker and discussed (optionally) by those who share in the meeting.]

There is no crosstalk at these meetings – which means we refrain from commenting, criticizing, giving advice or editorializing on what others share in the meeting – to ensure a safe environment for everyone.

It is customary to go around the room at this time and introduce ourselves, using our first names only.

Ask someone to read the **Foreword** on page iii.

Ask someone to read **To Those of Us Who Are "New" to OCD** on page vii.

Ask someone to read **Some Helpful Suggestions** on page 195.

Ask someone to read the **Recovery Program** and the **12 Steps** on page 17.

Anonymity is the spiritual foundation of our program and a major tool in helping us feel safe to share our OC Disorder with others in the confines of OCA. Would someone please define anonymity? (Who we see here and what is said here is not repeated outside of here.)

The other suggested tools of recovery include meetings, phone calls, abstinence, sponsorship, slogans, service, literature, writing and prayer and meditation.

Ask someone to briefly explain a tool and how it's working for him or her.

The speaker begins the step, story, qualification or topic (approx. 10-20 minutes).

Open for sharing (participation) and suggest that shares be kept to a maximum of 3 to 5 minutes per person. We have found it helpful when sharing to stick to the topic of discussion, although anything may be said by anyone (please respect our 12 Traditions). Crosstalk, or giving advice, feedback or criticism in response to what someone has shared, is not permitted. However, the speaker may comment *briefly* after a share if he or she chooses. Members often talk with each other *after* the meeting closes.

TREASURER'S BREAK
At a designated time during the meeting the leader announces a treasurer's break. We have no dues or fees, but are self-supporting through our own contributions. We pass the envelope for those who wish to contribute. The suggested

contribution is $2.00. The suggested contribution to the OCA service office at Box 215 is 1/3 of a group's reserve. The literature person presents OCA-sponsored literature. The "OCA" book is $19.00 and the "Family Guide" is $10.00. Books are available after the meeting closes. The leader inquires if there are any OCA-related announcements. The meeting is resumed.

CLOSING

Ask someone to read the "promises" on page 34.

(Read) The things you have heard here were given in confidence and should be treated as confidential. The opinions expressed here were strictly those of the individuals who gave them. Talk to each other, reason things out-let there be no gossip or criticism of one another, but only love, understanding and companionship.

SERENITY PRAYER

> God, grant me the serenity to accept the
> things I cannot change, the courage to change
> the things I can and the wisdom to know the
> difference.

It is suggested that a meeting start and finish on time. Most meetings are 90 minutes in length.

Meetings: Some Problems and Solutions

The following are some problems and solutions we have encountered over the years.

You would figure that with a great fellowship and recovery program like ours that everyone with OCD would want to attend meetings and work on recovery. Well, guess again. Some people will insist on breaking the meeting's format by:

- interrupting others
- speaking out of turn
- crosstalking
- sharing beyond a comfortable time limit (usually five minutes)
- violating the personal privacy or boundaries of others

Our solution: our First Tradition protects the group's well-being, which is that our common welfare and unity come first. Disruption cannot be tolerated. If the disruptive behavior continues, a group conscience needs to be taken, and by group vote the offending member may be asked to leave the meeting either temporarily or permanently.

During group conscience or business meetings, paliamentary procedure seems to work well. Each suggestion must be framed as a motion, discussed and voted upon before another motion is introduced. Members should raise their hands and wait to be recognized by the chairperson before speaking.

The Twelve Traditions of Obsessive Compulsive Anonymous

1. Our common welfare should come first; personal recovery depends upon OCA unity.

2. For our group purpose there is but one ultimate authority – a loving God as He may express Himself in our group conscience. Our leaders are but trusted servants; they do not govern.

3. The only requirement for OCA membership is a desire to recover from Obsessive Compulsive Disorder.

4. Each group should be autonomous except in matters affecting other groups or OCA as a whole.

5. Each group has but one primary purpose – to carry its message to those who still suffer from Obsessive Compulsive Disorder.

6. An OCA group ought never endorse, finance, or lend the OCA name to any related facility or outside enterprise, lest problems of money, property and prestige divert us from our primary purpose.

7. Every OCA group ought to be fully self supporting, declining outside contributions.

8. Obsessive Compulsive Anonymous should remain forever nonprofessional, but our service centers may employ special workers.

9. OCA, as such, ought never be organized; but we may create service boards or committees directly responsible to those they serve.

10. Obsessive Compulsive Anonymous has no opinion on out –

side issues; hence the OCA name ought never be drawn into public controversy.

11. Our public relations policy is based on attraction rather than promotion; we need always maintain personal anonymity at the level of press, radio, and films.

12. Anonymity is the spiritual foundation of all our traditions, ever reminding us to place principles before personalities.

The Twelve Traditions reprinted for adaptation with permission from Alcoholics Anonymous World Services, Inc.

The 12 Traditions of A.A.

1. Our common welfare should come first; personal recovery depends upon A.A. unity.

2. For our group purpose there is but one ultimate authority – a loving God as He may express Himself in our group conscience. Our leaders are but trusted servants – they do not govern.

3. The only requirement for A.A. membership is a desire to stop drinking.

4. Each group should be autonomous except in matters affecting other groups or A.A. as a whole.

5. Each group has but one primary purpose – to carry its message to the alcoholic who still suffers.

6. An A.A. group ought never endorse, finance or lend the A.A. name to any related facility or outside enterprise, lest problems of money, property and prestige divert us from our primary purpose.

7. Every A.A. group ought to be fully self-supporting, declining outside contributions.

8. Alcoholics Anonymous should remain forever nonprofessional, but our service centers may employ special workers.

9. A.A, as such, ought never be organized; but we may create service boards or committees directly responsible to those they serve.

10. Alcoholics Anonymous has no opinion on outside issues; hence the A.A. name ought never be drawn into public controversy.

11. Our public relations policy is based on attraction rather

than promotion; we need always maintain personal anonymity at the level of press, radio, and films.

12. Anonymity is the spiritual foundation of all our traditions, ever reminding us to place principles before personalities.

The Twelve Traditions reprinted with permission of Alcoholics Anonymous World Services, Inc. The opinions expressed on this material are those of OCA only and not A.A.

How to Get in Touch with OCA

Our National Headquarters can currently be reached at (516) 739-0662 or send a stamped, self-addressed envelope to:
Obsessive Compulsive Anonymous World Services
P.O. Box 215
New Hyde Park, NY 11040

Anyone who has OCD who wishes to start a meeting in their area is encouraged to do so. Remember OCA's message is the 12-Step program and how it can help us recover from OCD.

A meeting place is the first thing a meeting needs. Public meeting places such as houses of worship, libraries, schools, and hospitals usually have rooms for reduced fees.

Finding people to attend a meeting is the second concern. The following is a list of ways we have found each other.

1) Contact OCA. Let us know where your meeting is and the telephone number of the contact person for the meeting. OCA can then spread the word.

2) Contact the OC Foundation. Although not affiliated with us, we have a spirit of cooperation in helping those with OCD. The Foundation has a list of people who are looking for a fellowship like ours.

3) Local newspapers have sections where "community news"or "service groups" are mentioned free of charge.

4) Contact your local self-help clearinghouse – let them know your group exists.

5) Contact professionals in your area who have OCD clients.

6) Put flyers in post offices, libraries, or other meeting places.

7) Be patient. Most groups have found it takes many months to establish a core group.

Additional copies of *Obsessive Compulsive Anonymous – Recovering from Obsessive Compulsive Disorder* can be ordered directly from us.

Please send $19.00 per book in US dollars (check or money order drawn on a US bank) to:

Obsessive Compulsive Anonymous World Services
PO Box 215
New Hyde Park, NY 11040

Remember to include your name and address with your order.

Shipping is included for USA and Canadian delivery. Outside areas add actual shipping costs.

Obsessive Compulsive Anonymous – 12 Step Workshop for OCD
Join longtime members of OCA as they guide the listener through the 12 Step program adapted for OCD. Recorded live at the Queens, New York meeting of OCA!

If you are a member of a new OCA meeting or if your group is struggling with the question "How do we work the 12 Steps?" these audio cassette tapes will help.

Please send $ __35.00__ in US dollars for each set of cassette tapes (check or money order drawn on a US bank) to:

Obsessive Compulsive Anonymous World Services
PO Box 215
New Hyde Park, NY 11040

Remember to include your name and address with your order.

Shipping is included for USA and Canadian delivery. Outside areas add actual shipping costs.

The Problem

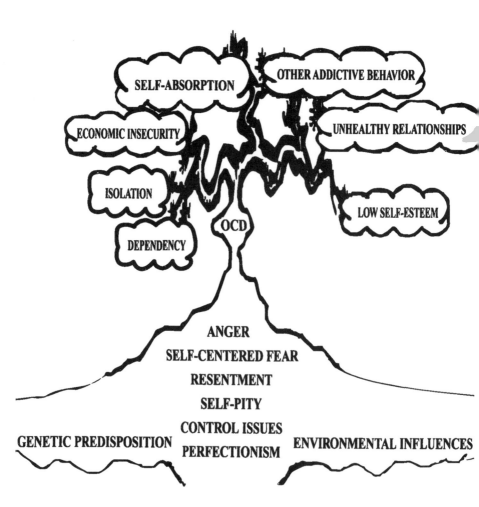

The Solution

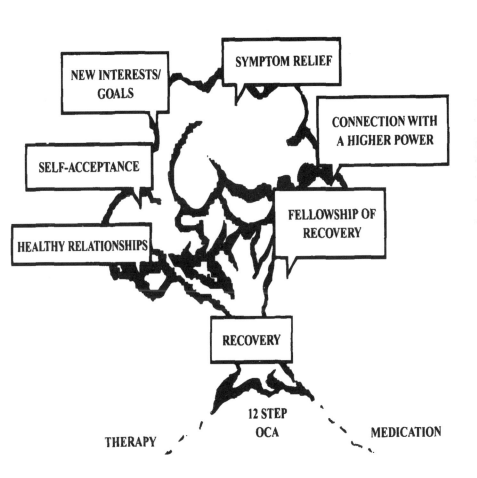

NEW INTERESTS/ GOALS

SYMPTOM RELIEF

CONNECTION WITH A HIGHER POWER

SELF-ACCEPTANCE

FELLOWSHIP OF RECOVERY

HEALTHY RELATIONSHIPS

RECOVERY

THERAPY

12 STEP OCA

MEDICATION

Resources for OCD

OC Foundation
PO Box 70
Milford, CT 06460
(203) 878-5669

Obsessive-Compulsive Information Center
Madison Institute of Medicine
7617 Mineral Point Road
Suite 300
Madison, WI 53717
(608) 827-2470

National Institute of Mental Health
9000 Rockville Pike
Bldg. 10, Rm 3 D 41
Bethesda, MD 20892
(301) 496-4812

Anxiety Disorders Association of America
11900 Parklawn Drive
Rockville, MD 20852
(301) 231-9350

Trichotillomania Learning Center
(Hair Pulling)
1215 Mission St.
Suite 2
Santa Cruz, CA 95060
(831) 457-1004

Hazelden Information and Educational Services
PO Box 176
15251 Pleasant Valley Road
Center City, MN 55012-0176
(800) 328-0098 (651) 213-4000